THE
KINGDOM WITHIN

THE KINGDOM WITHIN

A Spiritual Autobiography BY JESSE STUART

McGRAW-HILL BOOK COMPANY

New York   St. Louis   San Francisco
Düsseldorf   London   Mexico   Sydney   Toronto

Frontispiece by Woodi Ishmael

Printed in the United States of America.

1 2 3 4 5 6 7 8 9 0 FGRFGR 7 8 3 2 1 0 9

LIBRARY OF CONGRESS CATALOGING IN PUBLICATION DATA
Stuart, Jesse,
    The kingdom within.
    1. Stuart, Jesse, 1907–   —Biography. 2. Authors,
American—20th century—Biography.   I. Title.
PS3537.T92516Z523   818′.5′209 [B]   78-26481
ISBN 0-07-062224-8

Book design by Marsha Picker.

To Deane with Love

Books by Jesse Stuart

MAN WITH A BULL-TONGUE
   PLOW
HEAD O' W-HOLLOW
TREES OF HEAVEN
MEN OF THE MOUNTAINS
TAPS FOR PRIVATE TUSSIE
MONGREL METTLE
ALBUM OF DESTINY
FORETASTE OF GLORY
TALES FROM THE PLUM GROVE
   HILLS
THE THREAD THAT RUNS SO
   TRUE
HIE TO THE HUNTERS
CLEARING IN THE SKY
KENTUCKY IS MY LAND
THE GOOD SPIRIT OF LAUREL
   RIDGE
THE YEAR OF MY REBIRTH
PLOWSHARE IN HEAVEN
GOD'S ODDLING
HOLD APRIL
A JESSE STUART READER
SAVE EVERY LAMB
DAUGHTER OF THE LEGEND
MY LAND HAS A VOICE
MR. GALLION'S SCHOOL
COME GENTLE SPRING
COME BACK TO THE FARM
DAWN OF REMEMBERED SPRING
BEYOND DARK HILLS
THE LAND BEYOND THE RIVER
32 VOTES BEFORE BREAKFAST
THE WORLD OF JESSE STUART:
   SELECTED POEMS
UP THE HOLLOW FROM
   LYNCHBURG
THE KINGDOM WITHIN

For Boys and Girls

PENNY'S WORTH OF CHARACTER
THE BEATINEST BOY
RED MULE
THE RIGHTFUL OWNER
ANDY FINDS A WAY
OLD BEN
A RIDE WITH HUEY THE
   ENGINEER

THE
KINGDOM WITHIN

The phone was ringing so loudly that Shan thought it would jump off the desk if he didn't get to it in a hurry. He did. When he picked up the phone he said, "Shan Powderjay speaking."

"This is your editor, Liz Wordsworth, calling from New York."

"Oh, yes, Liz."

"Stand by for some important news," she interrupted him—"news that will shock you! We have just received word from Stockholm that you have won the Nobel Prize for literature!"

"Ah no, my God—no-no-no—"

"Yes, yes, yes! Your success is part of my success! And your friends and publishers here are rejoicing with you!"

"There must be some mistake," Shan said. His breathing was coming to him easier. "My forty-seven books, which are often referred to as 'barnyard,' 'redneck,' and 'hillbilly,' couldn't win a Nobel. I am in pain about this. I feel distressed. When my early books were first published, some people used to hunt me like they hunted for rabbits and squirrels. They tried to shoot me. They put me in the hospital once! My 'barnyard, redneck, hillbilly' books linger on, refuse to die, and win prizes!"

"My heavens," Shan whispered to himself. "What a dream! Did the pain cause the dream or the dream cause the pain!"

Shan didn't want to awaken his wife Jean, who was sleeping so soundly, so peacefully, on the other side of their wide Lincoln bed. He had awakened scores of times before in the last twenty-three years on this bed always with a wild, unbelievable dream like the one he'd just had, or he was wrestling with a python in a rain forest in the Philippines or being attacked by an alligator in a Florida swamp —or he was climbing a mountain in Scotland as he had done as a young man. His dreams were physical struggles or mental shocks when he was awakened by angina. In his sense of humor he tried to discuss angina in an article in which he personified angina as his True Love, who was always with him and wouldn't leave him—bad girl that she was, he couldn't free himself from her.

Now on a little desk at the head of his bed he kept his bottle of nitroglycerine tablets handy so he could get to them in a hurry. These pinhead-sized pills, sweetish to the taste, were filled with potency. Just one under the tongue would often give him a headache. When he had to take two to ease his angina, this gave him a severe headache. When he had to take over two of these pills, the pain was worse than angina. But he had to free himself of an evil which kept him from breathing.

Then Shan had learned there was another remedy for angina. He was a long time learning about this one. It was big, overpowering Dr. Amos Boswell, six-four, three hundred pounds as compared to Shan's six feet, two hundred and twenty-five pounds, who stood towering over him when he said, "Shan, I've told you and told you, you ought to have Scotch whiskey in your home, take a light drink with branch water and a little ice! I've told you, and other cardiologists have told you the same!"

"You've been a hard patient to handle," he continued to berate his patient. "Once when I put you in Intensive Care in St. Ann's, the nurse caught you revising old stories your wife had smuggled in to you. I'd recommend two ounces of Scotch to you in four ounces of water with enough ice to cool—and as for you, I wouldn't care if you got so drunk you passed out. I'd recommend it for you! You damned dry Baptist, fifty-nine years old now and never tasted whiskey!"

"Of all five cardiologists I've ever had, you're the rudest," Shan told him. "You have a military approach to your patients! And you have no manners. But write me a prescription for whiskey and I'll get some and try it!"

"Prescription, prescription," Amos Boswell howled, clapping his big fire-shovel hands. He'd once played end on State University's conference-winning football team, and was an All-American. "Prescription! Prescription! Prescription! Hear that!" He was so loud all other patients in separate rooms up and down the corridor could hear him. "All you have to do is cross the bridge at Rosten—over to

Toniron, Ohio, go into the package store, buy yourself a
fifth, quart or half gallon. I buy by the gallon because it's
cheaper! So buy yourself a gallon of good Scotch whiskey."

"Write the prescription. I never want to be caught in
a liquor store without one!"

"What a nice alcoholic you'll make after you once get
the taste! I'll write the prescription all right!"

He wrote the prescription, which was in Latin. Shan
could read it all right. One year he taught a first year of
Latin class in high school.

Jean drove the white Cadillac with the blue-leather up-
holstering on the inside, as Shan was not permitted to drive
a car. Dr. Amos Boswell had given him this stern command. She drove down through Auckland, to Rosten, then
across the Ohio River bridge to Toniron. Jean parked on
the package store lot and Shan walked in where three men
worked behind a counter. He laid the prescription down
in front of a big, pleasant, moon-faced man. He picked up
the prescription and looked at it.

"I can't read this," he said. "What in the world is it?"

"A prescription from my cardiologist, Dr. Amos Boswell
of Hummewell, West Virginia, for me to get a fifth of
Scotch for medicinal purposes!"

"You don't have to have a prescription from a doctor to
buy Scotch in here," he said, shaking with laughter. The
other two workers who had listened to the conversation
joined in laughter.

"What is your name?" asked the moon-faced man.

"My name belongs to me," Shan said. "I can read your
Latin prescription for you."

Shan read the prescription.

Then he was handed a fifth of a good brand of Scotch for which he paid his first money for an intoxicating beverage. He had traveled the world over and had worked around the world with those who did and didn't drink, but he had never touched it.

Buying this first fifth of Scotch on December 31, 1966, he had learned to drink something not pleasant to his taste. He had learned to develop a taste for this ill-tasting drink. It had been and was medicine to him. After buying this first fifth he had crossed the bridge many times in the years that passed to buy fifths and half-gallons because they were cheaper. He had learned to drink a whiskey-medicine which, added to nitroglycerine, had helped to save his life on his fourth and fifth major heart attacks when he was rushed to Auckland's Kingston Hospital.

Now, sitting on the side of his bed in the darkness of night, with pain in his chest, his left arm and his upper left shoulder blade, he found the little bottle of N.G.'s on the desk. He could reach out his hand in the dark and feel them. They had to be close. These little white pinhead-sized tablets meant life to him. He had to carry them. His wife Jean carried them too, lest he forget them. He unscrewed the top, dumped one into the palm of his hand. He put it under his tongue. The sweet taste made him sick. He felt like he was going to vomit.

He had better have his N.G.'s close. He should never forget them. He had to learn the hard way, a strong man physically who could lift a dead weight of 400 pounds up from the ground into a truckbed at thirty-nine, one who at 225 pounds could run the one-hundred-yard dash in "ten flat" until he was twenty-eight years old. He had been a

man who had had a good fist and was never afraid until his
first major heart attack left him for eleven months in bed.
He had to learn to use his hands again. He had to learn to
walk again. He had to make a new life for himself. He had
to struggle from day to day.

There was the time when against his doctor's orders he
took his farm truck to the woods on his farm and hauled
home a truckload of dead logs to be sawed for firewood to
use in four fireplaces in his home. He had been warned not
to do this. He had angina so bad he had to stand when he
reached the front porch and his Jean knew what was wrong
and brought him two N.G.'s.

There was the time when he started to haul a truckload of garbage to a bulldozed pitfall on his farm. When he
drove to the end of his lane road, angina seized him until he
could hardly get his breath. He drove out onto the hard-
surfaced Valley Road, a road that went the entire length of
his farm, three miles, and connected with State Routes 1
and 2. Here he turned his truck in the middle of the road
and drove back to his home, two-tenths of a mile, where
he parked in the lane road and staggered to the house. Jean
knew what was wrong when he staggered up the walk. She
knew he had left his nitroglycerine tablets at home. She
rushed to him with two tablets in her hand, putting these
under his tongue, certainly relieving him and giving him a
new lease on life.

Maybe the closest call he had ever had was when he
and Jean had driven once to Greenwood. Jean had parked
the car. He had to find a restroom in a hurry due to the
medication he was taking. The only restroom in Greenwood free to the public was in the Greenwood County

Courthouse. He rushed to the Courthouse and there used the men's room. Maybe his rushing had caused this. He had one of the worst angina attacks he had ever had. When he felt in his shirt pocket for N.G.'s he had forgotten them. So he rushed out of the Courthouse to where Jean had parked his car. She hadn't carried his N.G.'s with her. She'd forgotten them, too. He walked to Heisel's Drugstore across the street from the Courthouse. He entered gasping for breath.

"David, an N.G.," he said. "If I don't get one in a hurry I'll be dead."

The druggist gave him two N.G.'s in a hurry. He put both under his tongue. He was soon relieved, but he stood there shaking. His druggist, David Necessary, looked at him with amazement. It was a close call.

It never paid to be without N.G.'s in Jean's purse and in his shirt's front pocket. It never paid to be without a bottle of Scotch in his home. He knew his life depended on both.

Now he put one of the little white pinhead tablets under his tongue. One didn't begin to ease the pain. The pain was growing worse. Then he put another tablet under his tongue. Always he used single tablets first. He knew how to do it. He had done this so many times.

This damn pain he'd had so many times, which had come to him in his sleep in his dreams, in the darkness of night, was a nuisance. This was Lady Angina at her worst. He had never, never been able to discard this bitch who had attached herself to him as a constant lover. But it better be love-clinging bitch angina than another heart attack!

How could he live if he were having another attack. As

experienced as he was he could tell if nine nitroglycerine tablets couldn't dispel the pain, then look out! He was told by his last and present cardiologist, Dr. Ben McAilster, after he had taken five N.G.'s for Jean to call an ambulance and get him to the hospital in a hurry. Beyond five he took four more for good measure, two at a time under the tongue —which didn't get the weight of two elephants off his chest—and then, to be sure and for good measure, he took two more under his tongue.

Talk about pain. He had never had in his lifetime more pain than he was having now! His eleven N.G. tablets, dissolved under his tongue, couldn't slow, or efface it! His breathing was hard! Would he live? Was he about to leave this world?

"Hell no," he could answer this question he had asked himself. Hell no, he wasn't about to die. Five times he had had such pain! Five times he had come through! Now, he knew he had the best wife, a childhood sweetheart of thirty-seven years marriage. She was almost a cardiologist herself, who loved him until she'd comb his tousled hair in public—much to his embarrassment. She watched over the food he ate. She carried duplicate medicines for him in her purse. She had driven the car and had taken him places. No other cardiac on earth ever had a more loyal, prettier and talented wife than Shan Powderjay.

And now he'd had six cardiologists—the first four of whom were excellent, the fifth a big and quarrelsome one whom Shan had promised if and when the time came he'd be leaving in a hurry. Well, he had left him at the St. Ann's Hospital in Hummewell, West Virginia, when he escaped Intensive Care and came home in pajamas and robe with a sixty-dollar taxi bill. He had had fourth and fifth heart attacks under his sixth and last cardiologist, a pleasant, brilliant, smiling and well-mannered Dr. Benjamin Mc-Ailster.

Could it be number six he was having now? Nitroglycerine tablets could shoo away angina—could bluff her and make her detach herself from her lover. Nitroglycerine tablets could not slow or even stop a heart attack! The pain was so intense it was a beautiful city's burning. Maybe, all of ancient Babylon's one hundred forty-four square miles of city, with the wall around it broad enough for three chariots to be driven abreast, all in bright inferno shooting skyward. It was even worse than what he had thought and dreamed from his Baptist mother when he was a child the flames and tortures of hell would be like! Why had he been born into an inheritance where his father and his four brothers and four sisters out of eleven children had gone of heart attacks! And on his mother's side four of five big Sheltons, his mother, five-eleven, 180 pounds, mother of seven; his Aunt Mallie, 240 pounds, mother of fourteen, and two of his three uncles, Uncle Mel, six feet, 220 pounds, Uncle Jeff, six-five, 320 pounds, had all gone of cerebral hemorrhages. These were allied causes of heart attacks. Jason, only one of his mother's brothers, had escaped. He had a kind death. He just went to sleep. And this was the perfect way to die. It was the perfect way to ease out into that eternity when one departed his earth! Could that eternity be called an unknown?

Then Shan Powderjay had learned something from his agnostic youth when he didn't and couldn't believe! He had doubted his mother's rigid Baptist training even in high

school. When he followed a street carnival, when he
worked at the steel mills and certainly when he was under-
graduate in college, he had tried hard, but he couldn't make
himself believe. It took that first heart attack, which put
him in bed for eleven months. He had time to think when
he couldn't use his hands for three months. He had time to
think when he was learning to walk again. He lost many
of a perfect set of teeth and he lost his toenails. His first
attack had been his worst one. According to statistics at
this time, his double infarct with grave heart damages only
three out of a thousand that had it, survived. He had been
one of the three. Shan had even written a book about this
one when he recovered so he could use his hands—so he
could use a pencil, using both left and right hand, for he
was permitted at first only a longhand page per day with
each hand. This was the time when he knew he had been
spared and he became very chummy with his God.

This first heart attack changed his life so he knew he
would never kill anything that walked, ran, flew or crawled
except two poisonous, dangerous snakes. He had to change
his whole life plan from ambition to submission, from a
fighter—even with his fists—to one who walked away from
a fight and said a prayer for his adversary! A major heart
attack, a double infarct, with two arteries out and a much-
damaged heart, had changed his way of life.

Shan Powderjay had to have a God. He was a Christian
and he had the best wife, the finest cardiologist and the best
God in the world. He knew now that if he had lived in
Egypt in ancient times, Ra Atem, or Horus, both pagan
gods, would have been his gods. If he had chosen one god
it would have been Ra Atem, the Sun God—what a beauti-

ful god he was! He arose in the morning and came across the sky looking over his people living on the earth. At night he descended into the earth and visited with the departed ones! He was a beautiful god.

When Shan lived in Greece once he knew, had he lived there in ancient times, there was no question as to the god he would have chosen from their many. He would have worshipped the great Greek god Apollo. What a great god of Beauty he had been to influence all of modern Greece and to influence the Golden Age of Greece.

"Jean, Jean, this is it I believe," Shan said, speaking to her and touching her gently in her peaceful sleep. "Only one more chance! Fix me a stout Scotch!"

"What, what," she exclaimed. She rose up in bed startled. "What? What?"

She had heard his words before many times and she knew what was happening to him.

"What time is it?" she asked, sitting up in bed.

She switched on the light.

"It's four," Shan told her, looking at his watch. "Pain is threatening my breath! Pain is about to take my breath! Two elephants are here again—I have woven wire cables across my chest—with the weight of an elephant on each side pulling down! Jean, all of Babylon is on fire! It's going up in flames. My God, fix a Scotch for me! You know how! You've done it before! Don't spare the Scotch! Maybe, Jean, I won't have to go! I hope not! I don't want to go again! I don't want to go again!"

Jean arose from bed in her pink gown that swept around her feet. She rushed to a cupboard, found a bottle and Scotch. She knew how to fix it: two parts Scotch, one part water from the well—with soft water (branch water) and small squares of ice to cool so he could drink it! She came with a tall glass!

"I don't want you drunk," she said. "Don't drink it too fast!"

"Drunk or sober, anything to kill this pain," he said. "It's almost more than I can bear! It's taking my breath. It is worse than a fiery Baptist hell! There's not anything worse than what I'm having—not any kind of pain—not even when you gave birth to our daughter, Janet! May God be merciful to help me endure it. May God be merciful to help me weather the storm—even if I can and I have faith I can!"

Shan took one long drink. Then very quickly he took another.

"This on top of eleven N.G.'s," he said.

There was only his Jean to listen. She stood above him with a worried look on her face. Her big, big eyes were moist with tears as she stood there watching him writhe in pain like a blacksnake, about to die, stoned by people who didn't understand. The blacksnake writhed in its last death pains before its six-foot-long body quivered, then fell silent and lay dead.

Shan Powderjay was trying to hang on to stay alive and to get his breath despite the sharp razor's-edge pains that sliced his body to shreds! What the hell! Why did he fight back with the will to live? Why didn't he die and end it all? Others had done this! Why didn't he? He had the will to live! He had to think that he would live!

He took drink after drink from the tall glass until he had emptied the contents.

"Any better, Shan?"

"No better."

"Has the pain been lessened?"

"No."

"Has it grown?"

"Yes, it's expanded until I can hardly bear it! I believe my intestines will pop out! I believe my brain is going to explode and tear my skull apart in all directions!"

"What?"

"It's here! I'm sure it's here!"

"It can't be! Not another!"

"Fix me another glass of Scotch!"

"Oh, Shan! You'll be drunk!"

"My God—ease my pain. Drunk or sober—I don't give a damn—for God's sake ease my pain any way you can! Two elephants are weighing me down!"

Jean was like his mother. She was against drink—but not as much as his mother had been. She wanted to save the husband she loved. She ran to the dining room and got more Scotch from the Granddad cupboard—a cupboard 108 years old. She made a second drink, two parts Scotch, one part "branch water," water from their well—with pieces of floating ice. She returned in a hurry and gave the glass to Shan.

"I'm going to call the ambulance," Jean said.

"No, no, no. Don't you dare! I won't go in an ambulance again! I won't. I won't." Shan protested.

"But we must get help." Jean was near tears.

"The only way I'll leave this house is in the car with you," Shan said.

Jean knew he meant it.

Then, Jean hurried to the clothes press in their bed-room, largest press in their home, which spread across Shinglemill Hollow from hill to hill. They were the only two who lived very happily in this home. Pain struck in large homes same as it did in small homes. Pain struck to those who drove Cadillacs same as it did to those who drove flunkers. Jean quickly put on slacks, blouse, shoes and a sweater. She brought Shan a dark robe his sister Julia, a seamstress of no mean ability had made for him and had given to him for Christmas.

"How about the pain, Shan?"

"It's the same if not worse."

"We have to be on our way!"

"My God," Shan groaned in pain. "It's my sixth!"

Jean's face, always pretty to Shan, looked drawn now. Her large, blue-green eyes were misty with irrepressible tears.

"This pain is killing me!"

She took him by the arm so he wouldn't fall face down-ward. He was bent over, writhing in pain like he had seen a blacksnake in the spring trying to cross a highway which was run over by an automobile. The middle of its body was squashed by wheels and its head and tail were still writh-ing—but it was a reptile that had to die.

This scene flashed through his mind of that pretty blacksnake he had seen on a sunny day six days ago on the Womack Hollow Road. His Jean drove over the wounded snake. He wondered if she should have driven over its head and ended its suffering. It was such a pretty reptile with shining black skin on its back, white skin on its belly and throat, and the most ancient living survivor, older than man, upon this earth. Shan took down a note to write a poem on the resurrection of a snake. What a feeling he had, how deeply he was emotionally stirred after he had seen this. His Jean was stirred too and she drove on and the two remained silent until they had driven the three miles to Greenwood.

"Can you stand alone until I get the garage door up and back the car out?"

"I think I can! Yes, I can do—anything if I can endure such pain!"

She let loose of his arm. She raised the garage door, which was quite a lift for her. This was something Shan had always done. Shan tried to stand up straight despite his chest pains and the pain in his left arm down to his fingers seemed to circle back to his shoulder blade! He lifted the glass and sipped! Maybe this sip after sip of Scotch plus all the N.G.'s he'd taken would lessen the pain.

Maybe the combination of N.G.'s and two glasses of Scotch would stop the pain before he got to the hospital! Would death be better? was a quick question in his mind. A second quick thought in his mind answered that question. Hell, no, death would not be better than life. Another quick question: How did he know? He had never gone "beyond The Gate" to see if there were life beyond—to experience another new and exciting adventure! Was there life beyond the grave?

Well, come what may—Shan knew the pain he was having was his sixth major heart attack in the last twenty-three years. This heart attack was causing him to have such thoughts. He could die on his way to he hospital. Yes, he could die. He knew death was as natural as birth. He knew he had to die sometime. He wasn't afraid to die! He didn't want to die. Nearing his three-score years and ten, he wanted to live another three-score years and ten to make him six-score years and twenty! Life had been for him such an exciting, adventurous and precious thing! The greatest thing ever to happen to him was he had been born.

Even Methuselah's nine hundred sixty-two years, longest recorded age of man, had not been long enough to live and enjoy all the benefits that came from life and living. The reverence for all life he had and this was a religion! It was one of the greatest joys on earth. Thoughts came many and fast while Jean backed the car from the garage. In a hurry she got out, with lights on and motor running. She pulled the garage door down. She had to do everything while Shan stood there with glass in hand. She opened his car door. She came and helped him to the other side and inside the car.

"We don't have time for an ambulance!"

"No, not Big Thomas again! Not Big Thomas! Not his helper, King, either! Too many times and places in twenty-three years they've hauled me with sirens screaming —ninety miles an hour over crooked roads!"

Shan was speaking with half words. He was groaning and groaning his words! He was speaking when short of breath with hard-breathed wind from his deep-set chest in front of his broad, thick shoulders. He was now so filled with pain it was most difficult to contract chest muscles in breathing. He hoped his breath didn't get shorter! If it got much shorter he would die.

"Shan, I didn't hear all the last things you said for I was going around and getting in on my side of the car but don't repeat what you said," Jean told him as she backed the car down the drive.

The car jumped like a rabbit chased by hounds. It went like the worn-slick runners of a sled over packed winter snow down the steep winter hill where he used to ride as a boy in the winter of 1917–18.

Now, on this same hill on this fifth of April morning, minutes after four a.m., two rows of golden daffodils were lifting their golden heads. Between the two rows of golden daffodils was a winding little walk of concrete steps Shan had built up to an outdoor grill where Jean and their daughter Janet had often cooked. They had eaten meals up there where they could look down the valley at the exquisite coming of flowers, buds and leaves in April. They could see greening of meadows in spring. In summer they watched fireflies over the meadows. They heard grasshoppers, katydids and cicadas, songs on summer afternoons and evenings. Looking down the valley from this hill they could see the late autumn flowers bloom, changing from green to multi-colored. They could be a part of the flying leaves in October winds. They had even cooked out here in winter. This had been a choice spot in their lives. Even the April daffodils, he thought, bowed their heads to him as he was leaving them, maybe, forever!

Now the bright lights were on two rows of blooming daffodils—not always straight parallel rows—but slightly staggered from the house alongside their lane down two-tenths of a mile to the Valley Road. They were on Shan's side of the car nodding and bowing their farewells to him as Jean was driving at a speed unsafe for this narrow bending lane road.

On Jean's side of the car were the meadows now green-
ing-up with spring. These meadow bottoms were separated
by streams. On either side of the meadow bottoms were timbered slopes. Here stood the silent naked trees in a variety
of species all living together, growing and faring well. Shan
had memorized these trees in all their changing seasons.
These trees were loved by him so much he wouldn't cut a
single one. To cut a tree was death for it. He knew trees
had to be and should be cut for the benefit of humanity,
but not his trees. This was his reverence for life, for what
belonged to him. All of what he was seeing and loved
would be under his control as long as he lived. He looked
left and right at his valley he possessed by deed as Jean
overshot the turn at the end of the lane. She had to back up.
Then, she moved, too fast again. The white Cadillac split
the curves, throwing its bright lights like shafts of gold
piercing the four o'clock morning darkness.

Pain was more intense in Shan's thick old-muscular
chest where hair had turned from black to white. His
breath was coming harder. His rib cage was caving in. He
was writhing in pain equally as much as the blacksnake he
had seen run over by a car in the middle of its six-foot-long
body.

He put the glass to his mouth for another sip of Scotch.

"I hope it doesn't make you drunk!"

"Drunk or sober—whatever will kill this pain!"

"I know, Shan! I know! I've seen you in pain before.
I know!"

"I don't think you or anyone else has ever had to endure
such pain!"

"Birth pains are bad."

"If I were a woman and childbirth was pain like this, I'd never have a child!"

His voice was in gasps and sputters.

Taking in both sides of the road down the valley the land on either side belonged to Jean and Shan. They were leaving their valley full speed. Maybe Shan was leaving it for his last time. He looked painfully at his greening meadows. Maybe both Jean and Shan were leaving their valley and home the last time the way she was driving. Never had an ambulance, with Big Thomas or King at the wheel, driven him this fast. Jean could drive anything. She's driven over all the continental United States and through all of the large cities. She's driven tractors, trucks and she'd driven in Iran on the road from Shiraz to Teheran. She had driven a car in Cairo, Egypt.

Shan wondered if she would make "dead man's curve" on Valley Road. The big car swerved and slid but she gripped the steering wheel and got it lined up straight for the modest hill ahead. She was driving faster than Lawrence of Arabia was on his motorcycle when he was killed. Shan remembered the movie which he had seen six times. Jean could wreck and kill them both. Maybe his drink was affecting him. His second glass was halfway down. She drove by the settlement of Shan's people, where his sister, two nieces and two nephews had homes. At this morning hour, there were no lighted windows in any house.

She rounded the last Valley Road curve. Above this curve there was a city of the pioneer dead. This was Pioneer Hill, where all were sleeping, many of whom were Shan's boyhood friends. They had gone too young. They had not been aware of what lay beyond The Gate.

Jean reached the intersection where Valley intersected with State 1. She didn't look right or left. She pulled out onto 1 and their car seemed to be on the right front and right rear wheels. There were no lights in the windows of the houses and no cars on the roads. Their car, a long white mechanical ghost, was following its two penetrating bright shafts of golden light. Jean sped down State 1. Unlike Heaven's latest neophyte, she hadn't signaled left and then turned right. She hadn't signaled since she got in the car and started with Shan to Kingston Hospital.

Two miles of broad State 1. No traffic! Maybe, a minute and ten seconds later she had reached U.S. 23 where the signal light at the intersection was against her. There was no traffic at this time. Without a halt, but on the right front and right rear wheels, she made the curve to go east. She was driving so fast she swung over into the lanes going west. Then, she circled back to lanes going east to Auckland.

"My God—this pain!"

Shan took another sip of Scotch whiskey. It was going down in this second tall glass. It was medicine. Maybe, it would lessen the pain. Maybe it would ease the pain. Maybe it would do something!

"Hold on to life if you can, Shan. I'll get you there!"

He looked at the speedometer. She was driving over one hundred twenty miles per hour—on the two lanes east, broad, straight and smooth. If it were overcast or if there were stars in the sky Shan wasn't curious enough now to observe from his window. He looked ahead through his bifocals—he'd gone from 20–20 vision at forty-six until he could hardly walk without them after all the heart attacks he'd had. Were his once-eagle eyes going now? Would he be blind?

To hell and be damned with it!

He didn't speak his thoughts now. He gritted his teeth! He held his short breath then and tried to catch more air. He pretended to lunge for more air like the speeding car was lunging, splitting the wind! On either side of the car the wind was swirling. Their fast white mechanical ghost with the bright golden eyes had wounded the wind. It was fending for itself out there in the void of blue-dark night!

Rutland he knew and the red light was on their side of U.S. 23. Jean could see it. There was not a car on either side of U.S. 23 waiting to cross. It would have been too bad if a car had passed in front of her. She was driving over one hundred miles per hour—up Rutland Hill, over the top—through West Rosten—and through the red light at Rosten! No car lights on either side. Jean should have been an ambulance driver, Shan thought. If he got killed it would end the pain. So what—so what! He took a little sip! He tried to make it last until they got to the hospital. Maybe they wouldn't get to the hospital.

"I'm in pain. Drive! Drive! Drive! I don't care! Drive!"

"This is all this car will do! Auckland is close!"

"It had better be!"

They were now going past the Auckland Steel Mill and here were the first lights Shan had seen. The lights were in the mills and not from cars! Now the east lanes went around a slope, topped a hill from where they could see the street lights of Auckland.

"It's the last," Shan sighed.

He had drained the glass.

"Are you wide awake?"

"As much as I ever was in my life with this—continued pain. I can't take much more. If I give up now I'll die!"

"We should have come in the ambulance," Jean said.

Shan was getting short breaths. He was almost like a fish out of water. He thought of the fish he'd seen pulled up in nets from the Firth of Forth in Scotland when he lived there. He remembered how their gills worked automatically as they tried to breathe.

Jean came to a green light on Main Street—then a red light—both were the same. She drove high speed through them but not as fast as she'd driven on State 1 and U.S. 23. She turned west on Hospital Street on right front and rear wheels. Tires screamed against the concrete. This street crossed Auckland east to west—about six north-to-south streets intersected and the intersections were regulated with stop lights. Red or green, Jean was color blind. She must have driven as fast over Hospital Street as any ambulance driver who had rushed the dying this way. Big Thomas and King had brought Shan this way almost three years ago with sirens screaming.

Jean pulled the white Cadillac on the east end of the Kingston Hospital's emergency loading and unloading ramp. Here the patients were taken in when they arrived. Here they were rushed through in emergencies. Jean came to a sudden stop by skidding the wheels and leaving rubber tracks!

Twenty miles, twelve minutes!

"Pain lessened?"

"It's still with me!"

Jean got out and opened Shan's door.

"Hurry, emergency," Jean shouted.

There were four hospital attendants dressed in white who were at the entrance. One was a large woman who called out, "Jean."

"Betty O'Bryan! It's Shan again! He's in the car! Help fast! Fast! Fast!"

Betty O'Bryan went to the same little church in Greenwood that Jean and Shan attended.

Four attendants came running. One carried a stretcher.

"My God, the pain," Shan said. He was gasping for breath like the fish he had seen in Scotland trying to flip back into the water so they could breathe.

Shan left his empty glass on the floor. He was groggy. He could hardly see! His 225 pounds and all six feet of him was solid pain. Since his trouble started in bed, his waking from such fantastic unbelievable dreams, time didn't matter. He had been as near to unbearable pain as he had ever experienced!

"The sixth and worst," he sighed as the four attendants took him from the car, laid him on the stretcher and were off running.

"I never thought I'd be here again," Shan thought, but didn't speak his thoughts.

They carried him through the door of the Kingston Hospital in Auckland.

The place one should come when near death, Shan thought. Maybe, it's the place to come to die! Maybe, just die and get rid of the two elephants bearing their weight down on the rope across his chest.

He thought the rope was cutting him in half like the

careless mean driver in the car on the Womack Hollow
Road had crushed the six-foot-long, beautiful blacksnake
when it was just resurrected from winter sleep—just up
from the earth after the coldest winter in a hundred years
—so full of life, in his shiny dark skin on top and his shiny
white skin on his throat, underjaws and belly.

Shan's mind was getting uneven, groggy. Large Betty
O'Bryan, as lovely and good as she was big, was on one
side of the stretcher. Had she a smaller body it wouldn't
have held all her goodness. How lucky for him the four
attendants were standing at the hospital door with a
stretcher waiting for him.

On the other side of Shan on the elevator was Jean.

"Twenty miles, twelve minutes." She should be driving
Big Thomas' Greenwood County Ambulance. She was the
closest human being to him on earth—closer than daughter,
Janet, whom they had created jointly—closer to him, he
thought as he was riding on silken splendor—closer than
his brother, sisters, nieces, nephews. At sixty-nine, relatives from his family tree went down, spread out, in all
directions through layers of earth farther and farther from
the parental tree. They got weaker and sometimes wiser.
For out there with the black, coarse hair and high cheek
bones, there was the yellowish fine cornsilk hair too. There
were the trained and untrained, wise and dumb—far out,
far in—masculine, feminine and neuter genders. They
were something! But, his Jean was something else, beautiful, tall, slender, smart, a will to work, so beautiful to love.
She was durable! She was something! She was the greatest!

"Twenty miles in twelve minutes!"

She'd got him there! She put him on a soft bed with a

soft mattress, springy springs, and silken covers! Where was his pain! Was he awake? Was he asleep and dreaming? Or had the eleven nitroglycerine tablets and two glasses of ice-cooled branch-watered Scotch made him pass out? It better not have made him pass out—that stuff he'd not tasted for the first fifty-nine years of his life but took now for medicinal purposes because it had been recommended by Amos Boswell at St. Ann's in Hummewell—his fifth cardiologist who delighted in telling him his faults and needling him on each appointment. But Scotch had been a medicine that had dethroned him when he had reached an apex of thought, a brain that wouldn't rest before bedtime in his evening world. It was all that would slow him, make him get sleepy in his chair listening to a ball game on radio, watching one on TV, listening to music on radio, watching programs and music on TV. And a little extra, beyond what was prescribed, would put him to sleep in his chair.

He wasn't asleep, he wasn't dreaming, and he certainly wasn't drunk. Yes, he was that dry half-Baptist, as he had been called! He certainly was.

He never took his Scotch medicine that he didn't think of his dry Baptist mother and what she taught him! And he thought of his Methodist father, who never refused a beer or a drink of hard whiskey in his life, but Shan had never seen him drunk in his life. Why was he thinking these thoughts? What had happened to his mind? It was rational now, for pain had gone from his 225-pound, six-foot, muscular old frame, once a dynamic block of energy and physical power! When the pain subsided it left his body free! How had he been freed of his pain?

Shan knew now how he had been freed of his pain. All

of his trouble had been in his head and not with his heart! No wonder he had been in pain! From each side of his head he could see men emerging. They were small when they emerged, then expanded rapidly to big men. His body was lying on the floor of a big room with white walls that had some resemblance to Kingston Hospital's Intensive Care Unit, which had been divided into units by little portable walls and curtains.

Shan stood back from himself whom he saw lying there on the floor while small infants came from each side of his head. They expanded into men less husky, as husky, and more husky than himself. Shan stood back in the room dressed in his blue double-breasted suit, one with a vest which he always liked to wear, white shirt, black tie, which he had tied in a good knot at the collar. He had always liked to tie his tie which he could do in the dark or with his eyes closed and get perfect length and a beautiful knot. He had a white handkerchief in his coat pocket. He was wearing black shoes and socks. This was the way he liked to dress to give a speech, to see a football game, even to see a prize fight and he was about to see the fight of the century.

He didn't count the number of large, larger and largest men that had come from the right and left sides of his head as he was lying face upward. The action was fast and furious. There were as many men as there are on two football teams, maybe some extras, on either side that clashed in a free-for-all, a knockdown and dragout fight—right there before him in the big room with white walls. Shan, who had been mixed up in a few fights in his lifetime, had always enjoyed seeing one more than he enjoyed being a participant. Here he stood back in the room, in isolation, without pain, enjoying a fight of between twenty to thirty men—knocking each other down until the last man left standing was grabbed by the leg and pulled down—and beaten on the face by a monster man lying there with fists as big as wooden mauls. His grandfather, Nat Shelton, used to use wooden mauls when he helped him cut timber.

How would this fight end?

What was it all about?

It had not been just one but two sources of evil for him. His head filled with such characters that he hadn't taken time to put down on paper is what had caused his trouble. If he'd put these characters on the clean white sheets of paper with a black felt-tipped pen—put them there in his handwriting that hadn't changed since high school days and looked like crows' tracks in the snow. His handwriting was crow tracks scrawled on white pages. He'd missed doing his duty which had caused all of this pain first then this fight. How would it end?

Shan didn't have long to wait to know how it would end. With twenty to thirty men on the floor beating each other, his cardiologist, Dr. Benjamin McAilster, dressed immaculately in a brown suit, a white doctor's coat, but with large syringe with a long needle entered the fight. He was on the top of the stack, moving among the men as if he had once played football and boxed too. He was shooting each participant with quick action—anyplace on his body— and as soon as he shot him, he fell limp on the floor and his fighting was over. He was taking care of them one by one in just a second or two for each man.

Shan's always being afraid of a needle caused him to back up a couple of steps. Despite the raging fight between

the two groups of men born from his head and his own
good cardiologist Benjamin McAilster's winning the fight
from both sides, Shan wondered what he had in his syringe
that was so deadly to knock each man out with a little shot!
Yes, he was afraid of a needle used by doctors, nurses and
technicians. For eighteen years he was on blood thinner
and blood had to be drawn from the better vein in one of
his arms before he had had a bite to eat, a cup of coffee,
even a drink of water. Thinking of the good breakfast he
would have after the blood was drawn was enough to compensate for the needle in his arm, sometimes a little and a
few times much pain. Now, on his arms were spots dis-
cernible above the veins that caused him always to wear
long-sleeved shirts. He didn't want anyone thinking he was
a dope addict. Right now this battle of the needle with his
doctor, small in comparison to these warriors he had pro-
duced, was winning this battle. This room was no place
for him! He wanted to leave before it was too late. He had
to escape! There had to be a way! He wasn't exactly sure.

It was just wonderful to be without any pain in his
body. He wasn't short of breath now. Really, he didn't have
to breathe. He could stand, see, think and not breathe. He
could breathe just as naturally as he always had. He could
be a fish in water or a fish on dry land. He had never felt
better—and he felt the great strength of his body he had
in his late teens, twenties, thirties and forties up until he
had that first and worst of all heart attacks, return to him!
As a well man he had gloried in his great physical strength!
He suffered fears after that first heart attack when he
couldn't use his hands and had to be fed and had to learn
to walk again. He had dreams of fear; what if someone were

to attack him and he couldn't put his 225 pounds, muscular and thick shoulders behind his fist. That was the old thinking of what he had been. He had to adjust to the weakness of his body, a crippled heart and soft muscles and now, even, his head, characters, escaping from his head, violent ones, he hadn't captured with black felt-tipped pen to crow-track on white reams of over-length paper.

Time wasn't exactly an element in his makeup as it had been. He wasn't in any hurry. Time was standing still for him. He wasn't standing still in time. The air in the room was like wind he could breathe. He was sure he could hold a parcel of this wind in his cupped hand. It had color, too! That poem "who has seen the wind, neither you nor I, but when the trees bow down their heads the wind was passing by." This was partly wrong. He had *seen* the wind moving and standing still all around him. It was shelled-pea-green, Mediterranean-Sea-water-blue when winds are blowing over strong enough to toss ruffled white caps eighteen inches high. He had to go. He had to leave. He wanted to avoid the mess of men sprawled, lying limp and motionless on the floor.

Doctor McAilster, smaller than any man he had knocked out, stood above them with the empty syringe with the long needle in his hand. He was breathing hard and looking over the men on the floor. Still breathing, these were the men he had created in the two sides of his head. His cardiologist Benjamin McAilster hadn't noticed him standing back of his prostrate body, now lying on a cot in the room. Shan backed through a door into a corridor. This was it! He'd follow the corridor! He knew from memory Kingston Hospital was high upon the hill west of Auckland

and that there were corridors and elevators where a man could walk away and get down into Auckland.

Shan knew after he made it down into the city he would take Thirteenth Street, or Bridge Street as it was often called now, and walk out to the Auckland Railway Station. There he had got on and off some of the finest passenger trains in America. He had traveled so much on trains, he knew the men who operated the stations—the engineers, brakemen and conductors. His own father, little Mick Powderjay, was a "railroad man" for twenty-seven years. Shan had written much about trains and the men who kept the tracks ready and made the trains run. It wouldn't be hard for him to get a ticket down on Number Seven, money or no money!

One thing: he had escaped Doctor McAilster and the twenty- to thirty-odd characters whom he had not bothered to count in that room. He was in the corridors that led away from the hospital; down off the high hill into the city. Another thing he wanted to do was to escape that Intensive Care where Big Thomas and King had brought him more than once in the ambulance with sirens screaming. It was some show which he heard while suffering that almost unendurable pain that comes with an attack. Against the weaker bodies this attack is like a white hot oven furnace fire in the Armco Steel Mills in Auckland touching the green tender leaves on a weeping willow tree. A touch of white hot flame that singes, sears and burns the leaf forever! The attack is the torch on the sensitive green weeping willow in the spring of the human heart. The weak, unfortunate, often have only one chance. Shan had always wept for them when he read the obituaries of so many of the young who had gone this way.

When Big Thomas and King brought him in October, 1973, he was full of pain despite his N.G.'s and Scotch medicine. Jean didn't take him to the hospital that time but she was by his side. She could only see him five minutes, morning and evening. This was his first time in Intensive Care in the Kingston Hospital's Cardiac Unit. Shan soon realized this Intensive Care was not just for heart attack patients, but it was a unit where all patients were rushed when old Death was waiting in various invisible forms. And Death here was often the victor over life. He knew he wasn't going back to Kingston Hospital's Intensive Care this time.

He would never forget his first twenty-four hours in Intensive Care here. Why had it always been autumn before he got worked up to such over-reaction that he wanted to read all the books in a library, write all the stories, poems and books? There were not enough hours in the day for him and he had ended with a heart attack. He'd survived three autumns since this last one and this one had come in April, month of beauty and resurrected flora and fauna of lizards, snakes, frogs and terrapins and a new life for people. Spring and why had this happened to him? Intensive Care for him now? No, not for him! He'd escaped from his room to the tunnel.

In Intensive Care here in October, 1973, he had heard and seen eight people die around him. He couldn't forget. No, never, never, never! He knew Death had power over Life—just give Death time and he always got his man or his woman. Death had a pair of keen, observing eyes. He had his sights leveled at all times on all people. Intensive Care in Kingston Hospital in Auckland in the fall of 1973 was one place he loved. It was the place he liked to loaf to see who he wanted next. That was one place Shan was going to avoid.

He would miss "Scrappie" Crovin who was his nurse. He'd had many nurses in his day in many hospitals but not one like "Scrappie."

"Scrappie" was Irish and Catholic and a beautiful widow in her early thirties. She got the nickname "Scrappie" from the other nurses. The name suited her. Shan never wanted to know what her first name really was. He had lain on his bed there and wondered why any man who had her would ever let "Scrappie" go. She had had special training for cardiac patients. Dr. Benjamin McAilster had trained her and other nurses for cardiac patients.

Then there was a large, older nurse who was light on her feet, who could wait on a number of patients at one time. She was called Sister. But she wasn't a Sister in the Catholic church. "I'm Catholic, I'm married and I've got eleven children," she had told Shan when he asked her about herself. Shan was amazed at her great speed for one so large. "I don't have to do this for pay. Besides having children, I feel I owe a debt to humanity. I must help people." Sister told Shan she never knew who her parents were. She had been adopted as an infant in Chicago—and her foster parents had taken her to New York City where she grew up and married. Her husband's work with industry had brought her to Auckland.

When Shan was put into Intensive Care in that October two hours had not passed before four hospital order-lies came with a man on a stretcher and they seemed to just roll him off onto a hospital bed by Shan's. There wasn't a screen up between them. Young Dr. Drexell Duf-ferline, considered one of the best and certainly the most handsome of all doctors in Auckland, a doctor Shan knew personally, came with the orderlies. This man was his patient.

The patient they had rushed in didn't last thirty seconds. Shan heard his last breath go.

"So it's you in here again, Shan," Dr. Drexell Duffer-line said as if he were surprised at his discovery. "I read in the paper about you. I've just lost my patient here. But he was an old lunger."

Shan never knew what he meant by "an old lunger." Shan watched the dead man carted out for one of the Auck-land morticians. Shan had only seen two people die before. When he was eight years old he had seen his brother and playmate John die at five years of age. And he had heard his mother's last breath in this Kingston Hospital after a cerebral hemorrhage. This had been twenty-six years ago. Shan was now older than his mother when she went through The Gate. He had always regretted seeing his brother and mother die for these were experiences he could never forget. Now he had watched his third death—the "old lunger" whose name he didn't know and didn't want to know.

Across the aisle from Shan in the big room was another heart attack patient. The man had had his first heart at-tack at forty-six. He was the same age as Shan when he had had his first attack. Shan knew he was over there just across from him and he was Sister's patient. Shan remembered the first evening visiting hour when Jean got to see him for five minutes that his neighbor and fellow heart attack patient had his wife there to see him. She was a youngish woman who wept at his bedside.

"Scrappie" Crovin, Shan's nurse, told him that his neighbor was the father of eight and the young mother by his bedside was their mother and that all the children were out in the waiting room.

Shan, who lay often wide awake and listened and observed until given medicine or a shot to put him to sleep, heard his neighbor, whom he never knew, for a false wall separated them. He heard his neighbor tell his nurse, Sister, to stop. "I want to tell you something," he told Sister. "I know I am not going to get well. I am going to die. Now that my wife is gone from this five-minute visit and I can't tell her, I want you to tell her for me that after our marriage and bearing eight children, I have not been loyal to her. There have been other women in my life. I'm ashamed of this, having the fine wife I've got. I must confess."

"I won't tell her that," Shan heard Sister tell him. "This is all over, and when you get out of bed here and you're dismissed by Dr. McAilster to go back, go tell your wife you love only her! It will only cause hurt and trouble if I told her you had been disloyal. I won't and I don't advise you to tell her. I'm a woman, a mother of eleven and I will never cause hurt! I want people to have joy."

"But I'm not going to get back to her alive!" said the patient to Sister, his nurse. "I know I'm not."

"Are you in pain?" she asked him.

"No, I'm not—not right now."

Sister was called to the bedside of another patient across the aisle from him, two aisles over from Shan, when he heard his neighbor's words, "God have mercy on me. I'm gone!"

Sister heard these words, too, for she came running back to his bed. In a few minutes he was wheeled from the Intensive Care Cardiac Unit.

There were screams of a woman in pain just behind Shan. He had heard these his first day and night in Intensive Care. The second day he didn't hear the screams. He was curious about them and he asked "Scrappie" who she was.

"A young woman of nineteen with clots in her lungs," "Scrappie" told Shan.

"But I've not heard her screams today. Is she better?"

"No, she didn't make it!"

"That's terrible to have to go that young."

Shan had never seen her. Now he wished he had seen her face just once. Things went on in this Intensive Care where Death's presence had to be felt by each patient!

On the second day in plain view of Shan on his hospital bed, he watched a doctor put on a special suit and a mask and go through the door of a closed-off room. Shan knew this patient wasn't a heart patient. When the doctor came out and removed his mask, he shook his head sadly. Death had got another man.

The second day a man of forty-three was stricken at the Auckland Steel Mill, was rushed to the emergency room, then placed in Intensive Care, two rows over from Shan. Death had eyed this man from the time he entered Intensive Care. And Death had claimed him for his own two

hours later. Death was too greedy even in this Intensive
Care where he could select and have his choice.

A burned patient, burned over most of his body, was
rushed in. With two doctors and two nurses around him, he
died in ten minutes. Death was reaping a rich harvest from
this Intensive Care Unit. Here is where people came to die.
What about "Scrappie" and Sister? Shan wondered. How
many people had they seen die? Death had to have an old
face to them, one they had looked on so many times.

Very few women were brought in with heart attacks.
But, a woman, maybe fifty, was rushed in in the morning
hours and placed in a bed across the aisle from Shan. At
this hour Shan was wide awake. Doctor McAilster, with
nurses Sister and "Scrappie," was standing with two other
nurses who worked in the Cardiac Unit. Shan didn't know
why the nurses were standing there with his doctor. They
were, he found out later, watching the monitor of his heart
beats on a screen.

"How's my heart doing, Doctor?" Shan asked.

Doctor McAilster didn't know Shan was awake. He had
taken them by surprise.

"Well, your heart has its faults," Doctor McAilster said.

"Well, I know that or I wouldn't be here," Shan said.
"Still it's a good heart. I talk to it and tell it that it is! I tell
my heart that it is my Mr. Life and I believe it likes flattery
—for it keeps on going."

Doctor McAilster smiled broadly. So did the nurses
around him. Before "Scrappie" gave Shan a shot to put him
to sleep he heard the woman in the bed next to his die, like
a flicker of tired muscles, a long sigh of her last breath going

out—a movement—a last one of her body. How easy Death could be when he called one of his own.

She had passed through The Gate, had left the world forever in an easy manner—almost without pain! Look at the pain Shan had had, twelve minutes and twenty miles coming from his valley home to Kingston Hospital. He had had the pain for ten deaths, yes a hundred deaths like the woman who was the last of eight he'd heard or had seen die in thirty-six hours in the Intensive Care Unit of the Kingston Hospital in Auckland. That was the reason he asked to be moved out to a private room.

Here he was again a little over three years later, but older and his sixth had been a much more painful heart attack than the fifth. He'd rather pass through The Gate than return to that Intensive Care Unit. He knew he had to get out. He had to flee. Hell's fire, he had to be on his way.

This corridor he was in reminded him of the underground corridors in New York and London for subway trains. It was not as large and it was square and well-lighted and without tracks and trains. This corridor was used for walking but where were the people? Six could walk abreast here. Shan stood alone. He didn't have a pain! He had no aches in the calves of his once-powerful and well-muscled legs. He got these pains when he tried to keep pace with faster walkers on city streets. Like when he was in Auckland and walked down the street with a friend and his legs cramped, he'd meet someone on the street he knew or didn't know and pretend he knew him or had made a mistake. He did this to stop walking, to rest his legs, to get rid of the pain. He would never tell his faster-walking friend beside him to slow down, for his legs were cramping. People who had good health were scary about pain! People who had good legs couldn't understand when another had such pain in his legs he had to stop walking. It just wasn't the right thing to do. It wasn't for him to tell his friends about his pains!

For once now, Shan was walking down the middle of a corridor and he was free of pain. He felt wonderful and well dressed in one of his old suits—dressed like he used to dress before he and Jean were married. Yes, those young and wonderful days of good health which he couldn't appreciate then. It took time, and more time to make him appreciate days of the past for he had been too busy all his life trying to make each day and each earned dollar count. He didn't want to waste time any more than he would waste money. He had burned the candle at both ends. Life had to count for him. He didn't dissipate in any way. A dollar had to count for clothes, books, food (never medicine which he didn't have to have) and land was grass and timber—not even an automobile which would grow old with rust and depreciate. Land would grow in value.

He walked with open hands at his side. His arms were moving like pistons. His steps were broad and even. He cut down the distance in the corridor by thinking about his own past. It was very strange, he thought, he had not met anybody on his way. But then he knew why. This corridor led back to Kingston Hospital and that awful Intensive Care Unit which he had just escaped! He didn't wonder now why people weren't walking back that way! Why would they? Since he was positive Kingston Hospital was on a high hill overlooking Auckland, he thought the corridor he was traveling in with great strides would come to a place where it slanted down the hill and there would be steps. He had had trouble climbing steps. First big trouble he had had was on the Island of Crete when he tried to climb the Quarry steps of the Temple of Lindos, the Beautiful, and look out over the Mediterranean Sea at the green rippling waters. His legs almost gave way. It was some climb and people younger than he who had never had one heart attack turned and went back before reaching the top. He had to rest, briefly, three times before he reached the top. This had been eleven years ago when he and Jean were living in Athens and their daughter Janet was going to school there.

Here it was. He had found the answer to the corridor no one except he himself was walking. The corridor ended at a big door. It was an elevator door. The elevator didn't go up any higher. He pushed a button and got in the empty elevator. It went down with great speed, much faster than the one going up to the fortieth floor of the McGraw-Hill Book Company in New York City, where he had often been to see his editor. He would like to tell his editor Liz Wordsworth and all the other editors about the speed of this elevator in Auckland. Maybe, it was geared for fast speed because it was taking people away from that Intensive Care Unit, where there was so much death and dying in Kingston Hospital.

The elevator slowed, then came to a stop. Doors opened automatically and he got off into another corridor much the same as the one he had just left. Still he had seen no one.

He didn't care to meet anyone. He certainly didn't want to see Dr. Ben McAilster. If he did happen to run into him, what would he say? It would take a long time to explain his running away!

Now in this second corridor which was about the size of the first one where six people could walk abreast, he found the walking was good. He found walking without leg pain was beautiful. His breathing, although he was walking, didn't come in gasps and half-breaths. He liked taking whole breaths with arms swinging at his side. How beautiful this walking was! How swift and how wonderful! He was leaving all his troubles behind in the hospital! They couldn't get him now! Now even Jean would be wondering about him.

He would tell Jean about this much later when he saw her. He walked on and on in a golden soft light and here it was again. The corridor ended and there was another elevator door. He must go down again. But this wasn't hard to understand, going down from a hospital high on the hill to Auckland, a city in the Ohio River Valley below! How many corridors and how many elevators would it take to get him to the bottom of the hill? And wherever he came out in Auckland, he would find Thirteenth or Bridge Street and get to the old Chesapeake and Ohio Railway Station where his father used to work. His father got him a railroad pass, one for his mother and for his brother and sisters where his mother could always ride passenger trains free and all the children could ride until they were sixteen.

At the end of this second corridor he pushed the button on the big door. It opened for him, an elevator filled with the golden glow of soft light—softer than the sunlight. This elevator and the first one he had just ridden could be taking him down through the hill. He pushed the down button and the elevator moved like the first one, first with great speed and then it slowed to a stop. The doors opened and Shan got off into the third lighted corridor. And he still hadn't met a person. He'd not overtaken one, either, by his fast walking. And this fast walking wasn't tiring him one bit —not on a new road, going somewhere! His body was without pain. Shan couldn't remember, for it had been so long, when he had walked like he was walking now without pain. Doctor McAilster had told him to take exercises by walking a quarter mile if he could and increase slowly until he reached a mile—even farther if he could—up to two miles a day to give his leg muscles exercise and to get the blood flowing better in his arteries and veins.

Shan had tried to follow his doctor's suggestion to take this exercise for walking came slow to him and people driving along his Valley Road where he had to walk stopped to talk and offer a lift. It was almost impossible for him to walk along his Valley Road or his lane road which extended a mile beyond where he lived. There were too many people who knew him and strangers who knew of him who had driven in to see his valley. He had made himself a prisoner who had to shut himself in, hide in his own house, because so many of the people who had read and owned his many books were curious to see where he lived.

He had enjoyed autographing his books for the people who had bought and loved them. He didn't understand all the adulation, for books were normal things, born from the head as houses, boxes, toys and farm and garden were made by the hands. But still, there was a limit to Kentucky hospitality; he and Jean needed their privacy, the same as any-body else.

Walking happily on corridor three, he was glad to be alone. There was no one to stop him. Walking was easier for him than it had ever been. And he wasn't a prisoner of his own making here. He didn't want to meet anybody. He wanted to keep on walking. He wasn't hiding anywhere especially in his own house to escape people. As much as he loved people, too many too soon got to him. They took him away from making every minute and every dollar count, except when he was asleep. Never was anything to be wasted.

He had to work for the night was coming, and leave his mark upon this earth—that his community, state and country were better because he had lived. All the acres that he owned were better when he departed from them than they were when he got them. He protected all wildlife and more birds sang just because he had lived. He had talked to all the species of birds adapted to his region and they had talked to him. They had sung their songs of joys and sorrows for him.

Ah, the third corridor seemed longer. But his fast walking didn't tire him. It was a joy to walk and to be alone with his thoughts. He was happy about the way he had lived in his past, certainly after he had had his first heart attack and had had a great rebirth in living. Since that great rebirth in living and sometimes in years before this, he had always been a constructionist, never a destructionist. To recount as he walked in this bright corridor was a joy! It wouldn't be a joy now to recount his life if he had been a destructionist. And would he be walking in this bright glow of light? At the end of this corridor there was another elevator door.

"Ah, where to now?" he asked himself just to hear a voice. "Another elevator for sure! Will there be another corridor?"

Yes, it was another elevator, all right. He pushed the button and the doors opened. He got on elevator number three, which was the same as the other elevator he had ridden. Now on the elevator, he pushed the down button. He looked more closely at this elevator than he had the others. There was no up button. These elevators just took people one way, a peaceful way, in a yellow glow of light away from that hospital and death. This elevator was the same as the others had been: fast at first, then it slowed, stopped and the doors opened where he could look out upon the City of Auckland, a city of people on the streets, of moving coal trucks and cars, and of stop and go signs. And down on his left was Lexington Avenue. He had come down through the hill through corridors and tunnels to get here. It had been a delightful walking journey.

Walking down Lexington Avenue to Bridge Street people he met didn't see him. But he saw them! If they saw him they paid him no mind, not even enough to speak. He spoke good afternoon to a passerby, a man his age or older, who didn't seem to hear him.

Maybe, the man was deaf! This was a world with a new light after he got through walking the corridors and riding the elevators. Light over Auckland wasn't a cloud of smoke, fog and smog now. The afternoon sky was as blue as the wind over Greece and the Mediterranean—where cameras made the best pictures in the world. Greece was the only place he had been in the world where he had made pictures fit to be reprinted. At seven miles high traveling at the speed of 650 miles per hour, he had taken pictures from his plane window of Greek Isles in the Mediterranean that were later used in a magazine article he had written that was published. If only he had a camera now he could get some good pictures of Auckland and of the old Railway Station where so many people were waiting for Number Seven! Odd-numbered Chesapeake passenger trains went west. Even-numbered passenger trains went east. He was going for a short distance on Number Seven.

He walked down Bridge Street which extended beyond the Railway Station and on to the bridge across the Ohio River. Traffic on this road was bumper to bumper. There were some people he was meeting, people who never saw him but he certainly took good looks at them but he didn't know a face. Not one walking his way caught up with him. He walked past many who were walking his way. He turned from Bridge at Carter Avenue and walked down to Twelfth Street to the Chesapeake Railway Station in Auckland. Here he walked among people waiting for the train. They were people going someplace. They were people waiting for their kin, relatives and friends to come! Ah, it was good, Shan thought, to get back on the train. Shan walked among the waiting people over to where there was a line of people waiting at the ticket window to get tickets before the train arrived.

Same old agent, Bill Frost, was selling tickets. He had always been a master at his job—a man who could push a line and push it fast.

"Where to, Shan," he asked.

"Riverton," Shan said. "I'm going home!"

Shan had his billfold from his right hip pocket, where he always carried it, buttoned down. No one could slip his billfold out unless he unbuttoned his hip pocket. This would be hard to do for he could feel the touch of the would-be thief's hand. No one had ever picked his pocket and stolen his billfold.

"Here's your change, Shan," Bill said, giving Shan back three paper ones, a half dollar and a quarter, then Shan stepped back and let another up. He put his ticket in the front pocket of his shirt and his money back in his billfold, put it in his hip pocket and buttoned his pocket down. That was the way he had always done this.

He walked out in time to hear a bell. When he heard this bell at the railroad crossing, autos stopped on either side as the red lights flashed and the guard rails came down. Around the curve and down the tracks came Number Seven, a popular passenger train with a popular engineer, Big Lakeland Savage, wearing a pin-striped cap with a long bill to match his blue and white pin-striped jacket and overalls. He wore a red bandanna, almost as big as a shawl around his neck and goggles over his eyes to protect them from smoke and cinders. Big Lakeland always pulled his train looking from the cab window. Shan had heard him say that not once in his forty-three years at the throttle had he ever had an accident.

"Hello, Lake!"

"Hello, Shan!"

But there were so many strangers here getting off the train! There were strangers getting on the train, too. Shan didn't know a single face. The people didn't know him. He

knew Bill Frost, who sold him a ticket, and he certainly
knew Old Lakeland, as about everyone did, from school boys
to grandfathers, along his run from Charleston, West Virginia, to Cincinnati, Ohio. They knew his long white hair
flying from under his pin-striped cap over the red bandanna
round his neck, his face in the wind, his hand on the throttle, an immortal engineer who pulled a great train. Yes, the
people knew Old Lakeland Savage!

Shan didn't have any trouble getting a seat on Number
Seven. The whistle sounded and the people standing on the
sidewalks along the tracks under the metal roofs waved to
passengers on the train as it moved slowly from the station.
Shan looked back to see the guard rails go up and the
blocked road traffic on either side start moving east and
west.

Now old Number Seven was rolling down the tracks,
her whistle screaming for the many crossings.

First stop was at Rosten, a "railroad town" where Seven
stopped and people got off and some got on. There were not
as many people, though, as Shan had seen getting off and
on at the famous Auckland Station where he had gone so
many times and spent the night to get the morning four
o'clock train going west. Here he'd gone to catch the mil-
lion-dollar George Washington, Chesapeake's finest and
one of the world's best, going east to Washington, D.C.,
and then his pullman, going on to New York City! What a
beautiful trip that was! To think now of the food on The
George. "She's the Great American Train" which Shan
had written and had been published, made Shan hungry at
this moment as his train sped away from Rosten where the

largest individual railway yard in the world began and extended to Rutland. Also here were the Chesapeake yards where Shan's father had worked, where over five thousand men were employed now. Shan had once worked here.

The stop at Rutland was brief. A few got on the crowded train and a few got off. Shan was glad to hear Big Lakeland's whistle for Seven to be on her way. Here he enjoyed looking from his window at the farmland where April fields were plowed and ready for spring planting. It was good to see these farm fields again from the train window, land that hadn't been purchased for homes and acres for industry. Yes, Old Riverton was next! Here was the Old Riverton Depot where Peg and Old Brick worked. They were Shan's friends. And here was the octagon-sided post office under the locust trees where Shan's people, the Powderjays, had gotten their mail since 1896. And it was from here that Huey the Engineer pulled his little train, The Eastern Kentucky (E.K.) over thirty-six miles of bridges and through tunnels. Huey was a friend of Mick Powderjay, Shan's father. He was Shan's friend, too.

Shan had written about Huey the Engineer. He'd written two books about him. Shan, when a little boy, used to run to the Three Mile Station on his way to Plum Grove School to see Huey the Engineer sitting up in the cab of his little engine with a pin-striped cap on his head, wearing pin-striped jacket and overalls and a red bandanna around his neck. Shan and all the other little boys who went to school at Plum Grove used to run to Three Mile to see Huey, when he pulled his train in to stop. They spoke to him up in his engine! They waved to him when he pulled out of the flag stop. They wanted to be like Huey, grow up and be an engineer, wear clothes like Huey and wave from their engines to the people like Huey had.

Riverton, Old Riverton, a village with a big depot, a store, a post office and a hundred people, had been important to Shan in his boyhood world growing to manhood. Not many people had ever heard of Riverton, but the place had meant all the world to Shan. Small as this place was, a junction of Chesapeake and Eastern Kentucky Railroads, Old Number Seven stopped here. And Shan Powderjay was the only passenger to get off. Not any passenger got on. But here was Old Bricktop (better known as Old Brick or just Brick) coming out to meet the train. And here was Old Peg Stanton, telegraph operator, out to meet Old Seven and to wave to Lakeland Savage, a friend who was at the throttle pulling the train.

When Shan got off the train, Old Brick was first to see him. He spoke gruffly to Shan as he did to everybody.

"Hi, Shan!" he gruffed.

"Hi, Brick!" Shan replied.

Old Brick was bald with a rim of reddish hair graying around the base of his skull and above his temples.

Jolly Old Peg on his one artificial leg and one good leg, spoke warmly.

"How are you, Shan? So good to see you!"

"I'm okay, Peg, and how are you!"

Shan, Old Brick and Old Peg watched Lakeland pull his Number Seven down the tracks. Shan stood looking at Old Riverton. What a place it had been for him when he had walked four miles here over the hills and brought book, story and poetry manuscripts to post to New York City and other places in the United States. They had been accepted, published in books and magazines. They had gone all over America. They had been reprinted and gone to other parts of the world. What a place Old Riverton was to him! He was so glad to see it again. He stood on his toes, looked up to gravel-blue skies and he breathed deeply. Then, as Old Peg and Old Brick, his friends, walked back into the Riverton Depot, he was still standing on his tiptoes looking up at the skies. He held his breath. He had learned right here at Riverton he could breathe or he could not breathe! It didn't matter.

He followed the winding path where sulphur from the ragweeds on either side of his path used to discolor his pantlegs when he walked over this way to high school from early September until mid-October. But this was early April. The ragweeds hadn't awakened and shot upward from this fertile dark earth. From spring until early fall the ragweeds had been the most ambitious weeds, even more than smart weeds, horseweeds and jimson weeds, reaching upward trying to reach the sky above this path. Shan's path —a path that led him since he could remember, out from his dark hills to his destiny.

How great it was to see the old baseball diamond where he had played ball, with others from the one-room Plum Grove school, where Shan's cousin E.P. was teacher and coach. There was Big Aaron and Little Ed Coward, pitcher and catcher, Kennie Crown at first, Cewee Jackson at short, Cousin Penny Shelton, E.P.'s brother, at third, Walter Felch at second, Shan in right field, Big Timmy Felch in left field, Jason Larks in center. (His brother Poss Larks, fourteen, 200 pounds, could throw a sinker that dropped out of sight.) This team had beaten the older Greenwood High team in sixteen innings on this field. Penny Shelton, a left-handed batter was lead-off. Cewee batted second; Shan, third. They could always get hits for E.P. Shan looked over the diamond, just below the Eastern Kentucky railway tracks. The old diamond looked good. It was where his father led him by the hand when he was six to see his first baseball game. He'd thought of baseball as a career for he liked to play the game so well. But this wasn't his destiny.

His destiny, despite all the other things he had done, was to create people and to have them coming out of his head like had happened back in Kingston Hospital—a place he was fleeing from now. And he certainly had escaped pain. He breathed deeply and stood on his toes when he breathed. This was an old army exercise he had learned along with eight thousand other young men at Citizens Military Training Camp. When he was sixteen. Now when the air was cool and clean he could breathe deeply and hold the air for seconds in the sacks of his lungs. This was the reason he was barrel-chested and broad shouldered; even at weight of 210 pounds he wore a 52 coat and 40 trousers. That old army exercise of standing on the toes and breathing deeply had been wonderful for him from sixteen to sixty-nine. Nearly always when he climbed a mountain he'd stand on his toes and breathe. When he drove his car to a mountain top he'd stop the car, get out, stand on his toes and breathe. He'd look up there for a sunset or a sunrise. Up high like this was, it was God's world! That's why he'd always liked mountains at home and lived in them away— mountains in Scotland, Wales, Germany, France, Switzerland, Austria, Iran and Japan.

But on his winding path he didn't meet a person. Now to the Academy Branch Road where old Spitty Jackson lived, old Ugly Bird Skinner, Brady Callihan and Little Ron Banks. Ah, what a neighbor Ron was! He'd married Uncle Rank Larks' daughter Dottie, sister to Jason and Poss, with whom Shan had played baseball and had been friends with from children to manhood until the time, in a hurry, destiny had called him away from home, away and beyond his dark hills.

In the blue twilight, blue glimmer of April air—who could say the bluest air in the world hovered over Greece and the Mediterranean Sea—not a cloud, not a speck in it. Shan knew better now. He was walking in the bluest air, cool and right to breathe. It was the best! Better than in Greece and over the Mediterranean. It was here!

There was no one at Spitty's house. There was no one at Brady's house. Uncle Rank Larks' house was deserted. Shan thought he saw Little Ron Banks over on the right side of Academy Branch. He thought he might be going to check if he could see smoke rising from a fire someone had set. Little Ron was a watchdog about forest fires. One wouldn't more than start until he'd have firefighters there to stop the fires. This was why Shan's timber on his sprawling farm had been saved. Now he had the most and finest timber on any farm in Greenwood County. He had kept fires out by having neighbors like Ron Banks. He had never sold a tree. He had never cut a tree but he had set thousands. Very soon, after he looked longingly at Ugly Bird Skinner's shack up on the hill on the left side of Academy, he'd be on his way up the Right Fork on land that he owned, land he'd not seen for years because of his heart and legs. But he could walk this path now. Actually he knew he could run up the path as he used to do when he was in football training and walked this way from Greenwood City High School.

Standing looking up at Ugly Bird's deserted house, he had some thoughts about the cold rainy autumn and winter days, snow storms and deep snows when he couldn't make it home from high school. He had spent the night in this house. He had had the warmth of an open fire to dry his wet clothes. He had eaten food as good as he had ever eaten, here, prepared by Marth Skinner!

He remembered finding Old Ugly Bird alongside the narrow Academy Branch road many times when he couldn't make it home. Old Ugly Bird was a grave digger and septic tank cleaner in Greenwood. He made good money for his day and time. But there was one thing Old Ugly Bird liked better than the good food Marth cooked for him. Old George, the boot-legger, who kept Greenwood supplied with white lightning, never forgot Ugly Bird, his best customer, who paid him real cash after he'd dug a grave or cleaned a septic tank. Then, too, Old Ugly Bird liked some extra in his celebration of some deceased he was glad to see go, dig his grave, and get paid for it. A few of these, very few, had beaten Old Ugly Bird in poker games.

Once, just in time, Shan stopped a car coming down the road. He'd found Ugly Bird that September afternoon on his way from school. Ugly Bird's legs were out over the rut made by automobile wheels and his body was back in the tall ragweeds. Ugly Bird was a big man, six feet, 210 pounds, but Shan was a strong young football player in Greenwood High School, six feet, 180 pounds. He was country-boy strong, one who worked, walked, ran, exercised, who didn't smoke or "chew" or drink intoxicants. So he had no trouble lifting Skinner out of the road. A great part of Ugly Bird Skinner had been born and had come out of Shan's head. That's why he had been so fond of him.

Turning from the last long look at the Skinner house on the hill where there was no way to get up to it from the Academy Branch Road but walk, Shan hurried up the old path past Little Ron Banks' house. He didn't see Ron or Dottie as he used to. He was sure they still lived here for they were people who couldn't and wouldn't live anywhere else. Little Ron paid cash for all he bought. He wouldn't go into debt. He'd had the same house which he bought before he married Dottie. He'd taken her to it. His last car he had had for twenty-eight years. He'd kept it repaired and running. Now he was offered ten times what he paid for his car. Little Ron and Dottie had to be there. Shan didn't see them unless the man he'd seen climbing the hill had been Little Ron. The man he saw was about Ron's size, 120 pounds.

Shan couldn't believe his eyes. Ash trees were scarce in Greenwood County. But they weren't scarce on this part of his farm, which he had owned for forty-two years. This was the first farm he had ever purchased and it was closest to his heart. He had always been fond of this high hill, boney section, with the tall timber, a clear running stream, wild ferns growing by the cliffs in all seasons.

Shan had walked over this path on his way to high school, autumn, winter and spring. And he had sat on a stone and written things for his high school teacher's English class, once a week when written work was the assignment. What a wonderful spot of earth this had been to him all of his life and it was now. This spot of earth, his being on this path going up and up around the slope of the hill was a bit of heaven. Over all of the face of the earth where Shan had been, he identified with this part of the earth more than any other. His legs were strong and powerful. Breathing came easy now. Never, in any of the four seasons, had the wild ferns under the poplar, ash and oak been so distinctively green as they were this April. They were deeply velvety green, while the April wind, so clean it tasted, was that light-green high-hill April wind—such as he had breathed in many of the Aprils of his near-seventy years.

April! April! April!

Not the month of death as the two late autumn months and the three winter months could be and often had been. April was a month of new life and resurrection. Shan looked for a lizard sunning on a rock. He looked for a black-snake, as big and as pretty as the one he had seen run over by a car on the Womack Road. This was the month of resurrection, this wonderful April again! It was time to see a brown and black checkered shell of the terrapin who had just broken up from the soft rim of earth where he had hibernated—crawling with heavy weight on his wobbly legs —what a burden it had been for him to carry such shell for his protection which he had since earth was young. Back when he came into existence in a reptilian world, a time of the three-headed bat, a time of the big dinosaurs, who roamed the earth with such large bodies and little brains, the terrapin had needed a protective shell to be a part of such company. He and the reptiles were the oldest survivors on this earth. Shan liked to think these thoughts, old thoughts, how his beautiful earth had been created and what was left hereon. He wondered why his fellow man had appreciated it more and protected its surviving wild-life. He was proud that he had. This was one of his finest achievements, if he had any achievements; many people had said and written that he did. But this finest phase of his life—to create and construct and never to destroy the good—had hardly been mentioned.

Here were his gray-barked poplars, with bark the color of a gray squirrel's tail. They grew better down where loam was deepest, down near the clear blue water. Water going down, down, leaping over the rocks, throwing wet, cool-lipped kisses on the fronds of the ever-bound-to-earth ferns. Here were a colony of ash, butternut-gray barks without a bud or leaf, swishing their top branches as if to be waving to the blue April sky. Shan had watched a few of these ash trees grow since he was in high school. This was long before he owned this land. He had not remembered their sizes then, but he knew in fifty-five years they had grown tall from this loam, and with plenty of water for their roots to drink they were trying to reach the skies. When he bought the land he had kept them from being cut and hauled away to a sawmill.

Shan would not permit his poplars, ashes, oaks, syca-mores and walnuts to be cut for timber and paperwood. He had planted young seedlings in his forest where there had been spaces without trees. When his forests were green he didn't want any places where he could stand and look up at the sky. He had planted seedlings with a tree setter all over his forest. He had planted black walnuts and butternuts in the loamy earth to sprout and grow and make tall trees, to survive him on his parcel of earth. He could see the fruits of his labor here.

Sound of the April winds up among the barren branches of these trees was pleasant to hear. April fifth after a hard winter was too early for buds and leaves and early flowers. Even the stream which was now below him, singing almost as loud as the wind above him, would be mostly melted snow water coming down from the steep slopes. Wind and water made a world of music he had so often heard here before his legs had grown almost useless after all of his heart attacks. These attacks had kept him from doing hard labor, walking and running, as he had done all his life. Not anything slowed him now. His legs were active now. He didn't have any pain or shortness of breath. He wasn't carrying loads over this path as he once had, but now he felt that he could if he had a load to carry.

He remembered after he came home from college, in 1929 when radio was new, he bought the first radio ever in his county. The battery weighed 50 pounds. There was no electricity in the valley then, so he had to have this big battery charged each week. Shan would carry it four miles to Greenwood to have it charged. There was no way to have it hauled. His father never owned a car and he had not either for there wasn't any public road leading to his father's home. There were only three paths. The commodities they sold were carried out and those they bought were carried in.

The Powderjays and their neighbors loved music. Each Saturday afternoon late so many neighbors came in to hear radio music that the house wouldn't hold the people. They put the radio out in the front yard all summer and early autumn. They sat on chairs or on the yard grass and listened to music from faraway Pittsburgh, Pennsylvania; from Nashville, Tennessee; Clearwater, Florida; Cincinnati, Ohio; Chicago, Illinois; St. Louis, Missouri; Dallas, Texas—California, New York, Boston. Radio was bringing a world together even when Powderjays didn't have a road to their home because hostile neighbors wouldn't let them have a "wagon road." They had only paths to their home.

Shan's mother and father refused to move out into a world where there were public roads, free for people to ride over and walk on. He had carried on his back over this path, going out and coming in, loads of 100 pounds. He was thirty-five then. Produce had to go out and store-bought items had to come in. This path was the only route he had and carrying on his shoulders was the only way he had. Some difference from how fast he had got Jean to the hospital when their Janet was born, and how Jean had raced him over the roads twenty miles in twelve minutes to Kingston Hospital!

No wonder he knew this path so well, loved it so much! It was his. All of this was one with his flesh and blood. He had often wondered why other people didn't feel the same way. Thoughts returned over and over in his mind that in this oneness with their earth, their rivers, skies, mountains and seas they would feel much stronger. They would feel secure and as solid as their earth upon which they walked. They would be in oneness with their God who had always been. They were the dust of the earth made living through the process of God. They had rented the living dust which was their bodies. These had to be returned home in the end. After their bodies' extended use and their fulfillment, they returned to oneness with earth from which they came. Gray granite stones, sand stones, slabs or not anything at all could mark their bodies' resting places, but this didn't matter. This was only a token of where each person's enriched dust from earth had been laid back to rest. There were not even tokens for countless millions where the wind blew over and hummed mournful ditties for them.

He walked on this path around the side of the hill, which was at a thirty-five degree angle. Beautiful earth leaning up against a blue April sky that he was walking on. Below him now, he looked back at the valley and tall barren timber below. On all his fertile topsoil he had not seen any trailing arbutus, first wild flower to bloom; he had not seen his favorite white percoon blossom which had red coloring in its roots and was always second to bloom in spring. He had not seen in his woods along this path little colonies of May apples which came up from the loamy soil with their tops shaped like small green umbrellas. April fifth, after the hard winter, was a little too early for them. He had seen these flowers here on so many Aprils and he had missed them going back home. Shan knew where he was going all right. There was so much to see, so much to feel and so many things to think about from the past to the present, so much to love and enjoy, this journey home had been slowed.

Time wasn't an element, Shan thought, as he stood on the hilltop where there was a stile for climbing over a woven wire sheep fence. He was here all right, ready to climb over it. Here was the only place on his four miles to Greenwood he put the 50-pound radio battery down to rest long enough to climb up the steps, over the stile and down steps over the other side. He let the square-shaped heavy battery, awkward to carry, rest on the flatboard on top of the stile that covered the wires. He had other memories about this top board on his four-mile walking path to Greenwood. Here he had laid down loads up to 100 pounds to rest and catch his breath a minute or so, for he had always been in a hurry. There had never been time enough to live and to do all the things he wanted to do. A century was not long enough to live. One who lived beyond this age was like traveling fast enough to break the sound barrier—beyond a century of living broke the natural life barrier.

It was here when Shan rested that he often thought of poems he wanted to write. From here he could see over into the Ohio River Valley. He could see from his farm over into Ohio which had been a friendly state to him.

One other place where he had been reminded him of this scene. In the six square miles of Macao, an independent little island country with 300,000 people, he could see over and down on the People's Republic of China where there were eight hundred million people. Macao was non-Communist. Over *there* were the red roofs, red flags flying from tall poles. But over *here*, Shan looked down on friendly Ohio across the broad Ohio River. The river was a restless, rippling ribbon of light flowing through April's light green wind. Yes, over there across that broad river were friendly people. This was one world. But looking down from this high hill brought little Macao back to Shan, only a gate and a narrow body of water separating them, the elephant and the mouse.

Walking out this ridge road path, where pasture land flowed like green waters into trees in the valley and on the slopes—was a land that would remind the English of their English countryside. Shan, his father, his brother and some hired help had made this a beautiful land, first for sheep and later for cattle to graze upon and to love the shade under the trees. How great, wonderful and beautiful was the earth. Earth had been kind to man to feed him and sustain his life. In return, man should compensate with his love and oneness with the earth. Always to build and never to destroy! Look where he was now! What beauty there was in this thin green April wind's eerie light over the pasture fields, the leafless woods and little valleys that all came into the main valley.

Under a small cluster of oaks, Shan stopped. He had created many Plow people here. On an old log which lay near the woven wire sheep fence he had sat while he rested from walking to write an article published in a national magazine that was used as a chapter in one of his books and had been reprinted in textbooks. His world had many memories. His world had good memories. His world now was a time of things he had thought and written that were flashed as fresh reminders before him. What he had done in his world was returning to him.

It was so good to walk on this ridge where no later than last March he had driven in his small hill-climbing car. His legs were not good for hill climbing then. He had wonderful legs now. He had wanted to come here to see if his pasture fields were greening for spring. Yes, but greening very slowly after that cold winter. It was over the path he had come from the Academy Branch Road that was the main artery of travel. His mother, father, three sisters and his brother, walked four miles from home to Greenwood into a world where roads and streets were free. This was the path over which they had traveled and carried their loads in with laughter and sadness. This was their road all right. It was Shan's road now as it had been all of his life.

Ah, there it was, his home over there on the saddle between two hills. He was standing up on this high ridge looking down across the separate little valley he had helped his father farm when he was a boy. Here near the top of the hill they had set an orchard of apple trees. The rest of this valley was fenced for pasture for their four cows. And it was at the foot of this hill where the path went down in "S" curves which made it easier for climbing up the hill that Shan had found an albino blacksnake one September morning on his way to high school. He went back home with his snake to put it in a box for the day. Later he made a pen for it. He fed this beautiful reptile milk and table scraps until it hibernated. This was his greatest nature find. It had significance. He kept the snake all the time he was in high school while he searched for another albino blacksnake for breeding purposes. He never found one. He turned his gentle albino free when he left his father's home for a world beyond.

Now he walked down this curved path where apple trees were aging as Shan's body had been, over rock that cropped out from under dirt on the slope. There was his old home, four rooms below, two above and a sprawling back porch he was about to reach. Shan and his Grandpa Nat Shelton had built this house when Shan was fourteen and his grandfather was seventy. They had made a log house, a chimney up through the center with two fireplaces. His grandfather had hewed the rocks as he and his grandfather had cut oak trees, scored and hewed their sides to make pretty house logs. They had built a house while Shan's father walked five miles to and five miles from his work for a ten-hour day of railway section labor. His mother had taken care of the family and had done the canning to fill the cellar his grandfather had made of stone. She gathered wild blackberries, strawberries, raspberries and dewberries. She had canned and made jellies of these. She gathered wild plums and wild grapes and made jellies of these. There was the smokehouse over the cellar. There were the twin hickories in the back yard where she had worked under their shade stirring apple butter, rendering lard, or making lye soap in a big wash kettle over a slow fire. She had washed and boiled clothes here.

It wasn't long now until he'd see them! They'd be waiting there for him. Shan had always been close to his mother and his father. His sisters and brother had been close to them. The Powderjay family had been all for one and one for all. This was the way they lived. This was the way they could live in their poor circumstances which they loved and enjoyed even if the world about them was often a hostile one. Shan didn't stop in the back yard. He walked around to the front yard.

"Shan," his mother said.

"Mom," he replied.

"It's been a long time," said his father.

He was sitting on the grass just beginning to green under the poplar tree in the front yard.

"Mom, it's been twenty-six years."

"Oh, no," she corrected him, smiling a pleasant smile. "Not quite that long. Not 1951, but October 8, 1954. Don't you remember being with an angel in the pasture?"

"You're right, Mom," Shan agreed. He sat down under the poplar tree that had once furnished their spring, summer and early autumn shade.

And it was under this tree where they used to have the battery radio summers of 1929, 1930 and 1931. Here people had gathered Saturday afternoons to hear from other parts of the United States. It was here under this tree they had learned of that vast world out there. Many of their neighbors couldn't read, but now they could listen about that world out there. All parts of the country were coming closer together. It was here that oneness with the earth had its beginning.

Shan sat on the grass beside his parents Mollie and Mick Powderjay. Shan's mother never kissed him after their long departure, when she hadn't seen or heard from him and he'd not seen nor heard from her. She had never shown her affection for him nor his brother and sisters she had brought into the world. Shan could never remember his mother's ever kissing him. Had she ever kissed him he had been too young to remember. He had never seen her kiss one of his sisters or his brother or even his father.

Despite her not kissing him or his kissing her—and certainly in Shan's family fathers didn't kiss sons, sons didn't kiss father or one another—they were close-knit. Shan's family hadn't been a kissing family. There was the hearty handshake between men and women. There had been and was affection among the members of his family— affection strong, durable and everlasting.

Now sitting on the grass under the poplar tree, Shan shook his mother's warm hand as he looked on her smiling face and her April-wind green eyes—eyes not too large and shaped like his own. He had his mother's eyes all right—not his father's big blue eyes and his father's long Roman nose.

After his handshake with his mother, who always came first, he and his father clasped hands with a hearty and affectionate handshake greeting.

"You look well, Shan," she said. "Don't you think he does, Mick?"

"Yes, Mollie," he replied.

Shan looked at his tall mother sitting there on the ground. He looked at her green eyes, her big mouth that he had inherited, her olive one-fourth Cherokee complexion, her high cheekbones, her charcoal-black straight hair, done up in a bun and pinned on the back of her head, dressed in a familiar long gray dress with white around the collar she had made for herself—a dress she wore in later years and loved. She was wearing a gray coat and black slippers. She was still so pretty even if she were five feet eleven inches tall. No wonder his father had loved her though they were so different in dispositions they couldn't get along. Each one had lived almost in a different world for fifty years. And here they were together.

His father, sitting on the grass beside her, five feet eight, never weighing more than 144 pounds, was always a better dresser than his mother. He was wearing a brown suit he had always loved in late years, a white shirt, a brown bow tie and a brown hat. He had always loved brown. He was wearing tan shoes and brown socks.

"Dad, I've never seen you dressed better," Shan said.

Then Shan's mother, his father and he laughed together. This was such a pleasant getting-together.

"Shan, come Christmas it will be twenty-three years since we've seen one another. You had gone to bed with your first one."

"Yes, I remember," Shan said. "You and I had planned to get together, raise a garden. I wanted you to teach me what your secret was when you could always grow from the good new earth better vegetables than I could ever grow. You always beat me, Dad!"

Shan remembered after he grew to manhood there had been meetings with his father not as pleasant as this one was. His father's moods were subject to quick changes where he could become hot and ill-tempered—as fickle as the April winds blowing through the poplar trees' large arm-branches that tapered down to treelimb wrists, thumbs and fingers. The winds above them sang through these branches now. Yes, their house upon this hill was in the path of winds that blew from four directions, east, north, west and south. Shan looked up and around to see now, for he remembered winds that had blown roofs off the house, barn, corncrib and smokehouse. He didn't see any roofs blown off but there were four trees he could count in three directions with their tops blown down and broken by the angry winds that blew incessantly here. There was one oak he remembered so well that was blown over above the house. His youngest sister, Julia, had played with her dolls under that tree.

"It's wonderful to see you together and looking so well," Shan said to his parents. "I've never seen you in a happier mood."

"We're together, all right," his mother said. "We're together forever. There were times, as you will remember, when we didn't get along too well—but we couldn't be apart."

"We've had a beginning and now we have no ending," his father said. "We have gone in a circle. We began here. We're back to here. It's all a joy, Shan, this never ending! We lived right, Shan, in our different worlds."

"How's Jean?" Shan's mother asked.

"All right when I left her at Kingston Hospital. I had to get out of that place. Remembering the past, all the agony and the pain, I found a way out. I found a way to escape it all. I chose that way to escape the pain and a hospital room which can be a prison. And I don't like to see the people around me die."

"They don't die, Shan," his mother said. "They only change into something rich and strange. Can you kill water? Heated water goes up into the air as steam. It can be chilled by a wind and fall down to earth again in drops of rain. You can't kill water! You can't kill you! You are you, man different, living in borrowed dust! I am I—woman different—your father is man different. We are here. You are here. It's wonderful to meet again."

"How about getting up from this soft grass, going to the old well in the back yard and tasting of that water again," his father said.

"That would be fine, Mick."

His mother started rising up.

"Suits me, too," Shan said.

Shan and his parents arose from sitting on the dry brown April grass under the yard poplar with barren branches. Shan was an inch taller than his mother, four inches taller than his father. Shan's brother Jason was five inches taller than he. But, Jason wasn't here.

"This place holds dreams," his mother said. "Not one born of natural birth here. Not one ever to make the change in life, going through The Gate into something rich and strange here. It's a wonderful feeling to be here at this time of April."

"The well box I made with the windlass and rope," Mick Powderjay said to his wife and son. "Here's the sassafrass I planted by this well box to put a shade tree over this well. But, look up over this well there. The wind has broken the top out of it. Dave Thompson and I dug that well and walled up the circular hole with field stones. Old Ugly Bird Skinner found the vein of water for us here with a peach tree fork. Right here is where the fork went down pointing to the gusher vein of cold water and Dave and I dug down and found it—only twenty-two feet below the surface."

"Water we've used for drinking and cooking from this well," Mollie said smiling. "It's really water of life from our good, wonderful and beautiful earth."

"Mollie, we had a deed for fifty acres! But we owned much more."

Only Shan, his mother and father were back at their old home where Shan's mother and father had lived thirty-one years of their lives while Shan had lived nineteen happy years of his life. In all directions but one Shan had plowed the hillslopes with mules and horses hitched to bull-tongue plows to break the root-filled land. Then he had used the single-shovel and double-shovel plows, pulled by one mule between corn rows. His hoe had dug into the earth around him in all directions except one. That direction was out toward the old barn by the sandstone gap. A timbered hill stood above the sandstone gap and barn.

In all directions but one which Shan could see from this well, he had sat on the beam of his plow and let his mules rest and he had let the people come from his head out onto paper. The mules didn't know what he was doing but mules he worked hitched to his plow could appreciate him as their master. Shan was proud now that he had always been kind to animals as his father had been before him.

Shan had always carried a favorite book at the plow. Nearly all of the time, when he had them, he had carried pencil and paper. If he didn't have them, being a very resourceful boy and man when he worked, played and dreamed on his good earth, he could find a way to do the thing he liked to do best. This was when he had something in his head that had to be born, whether this be people or ideas, after short or long pregnancies, they had to be born. People that formed in his head got too overripe and they had to leave in a hurry.

The word was here. The word was the thing. The word on paper was a thing of forever, too. Shan either knew or thought this from the time he could remember. He had written a poem on "things that last" when he was twenty-four and his conclusion was not houses, cities, streets—even stones crumpled, but choice words and music would be the things to last. How could a word crumple? How could a word selectively chosen and properly placed embracing an idea upon its shoulder—or helping to contain a human character on this earth—ever die? How could Shan's earth ever crumple? How could the word be killed? How could music and the dreams be killed? Shan learned early about these things. He learned later about that something within that would not die but lived forever.

Shan had tried to kill his first book. How well he could remember this now. He was standing twenty feet away from the twin hickories above the well in this back yard. Under these twin hickories, in late summer and early autumn shade his mother had always made apple butter. She had raked up chips from the chipyard which was on above the twin hickories. It was here she used a second kettle to render lard from the hogs Powderjays killed for their winter meat. Also, in a third large kettle she made soap from the lye of wood ashes for them to use on their faces and bodies. For Powderjays, cleanliness was akin to Godliness. The cleanliness of bodies and clothes had to be. His mother washed their clothes with the soap she made under the twin hickories, close where they were standing. She always had a low fire under the kettle which was placed far enough so it wouldn't kill their hickories which were a part of the household.

When Shan wasn't in the fields, going to school, or away teaching school, he always joined in to help his mother when she worked under the twin hickories. Not any other woman Shan had ever known did more work under trees than his mother had done under these twin hickories. She would rather work out in the wind and sun. She preferred to work in the fields with Mick and Shan than to work in the house. She could use a hoe better than Mick or Shan.

So one day while stirring apple butter with his mother
under the twin hickories, Shan had an idea. Several copies
of *Harvest*, his first book of poems that wouldn't sell for a
dollar each privately published on borrowed money, he
brought down from upstairs. He brought down some copies
of a book he had paid to have published. He had given
copies to several friends who would accept them. These
were out against him. He was writing better poems now
even if he didn't have paper and pencils. He was writing
Plow poems on the innerside of the large poplar leaves
with a little sharp-ended stick. He wasn't letting the ideas
and images escape when they came to him. He was putting
people on leaves, people in his head, ugly, mean, wonderful and beautiful people who had to be born.

Now, downstairs and to the slow-burning fire under
the kettle he laid copies of *Harvest*. Not all at one time!
The heat might hurt the twin hickories. After the first
books burned, then came all the rest to the fire. This saved
more chips for his mother and for him in the chipyard.

Harvest was not good. Parts of it were youthful silliness
recorded awkwardly in words. Shan knew this. It was the
sounding of brass cymbals. It was the vanity of youth published by a vanity press. Shan soon got above all these alien
ideas and characters that emerged from his head. He got so
far above this he felt ashamed.

When *Plow*, his first legitimate book appeared, a block-
buster of earth men and women, beauty of the earth and
all the senses of man (except smell which Shan did not
have) his eastern publishers advertised it as his first book.
Shan had told them *Plow* was his first book. He didn't tell
them about his clumsy first book, *Harvest*. He didn't tell

them since they liked *Plow* so well. He wouldn't have told them anyhow for *Harvest* was as dead as yesterday's four o'clock. Were literary lies as bad as others, he wondered?

In all directions from this well with a broken top, with its twin hickories and sassafrass, were spots where Shan had sat on plow beams, under trees, on rocks to write on paper and leaves. His paper had not always been the nicest paper —not what writers usually used. Many men in his neighborhood chewed tobacco. When they emptied a paper sack of their sweet chewing tobacco—Shan's father, Mick, was one of these men who liked his sweet chewing—Shan picked up the sacks. He gathered them up from along the road. And his father Mick couldn't understand when he tore apart the sack which had an inner and outer side. Shan would get six to eight poems on one of these sacks— poems fourteen to sixteen lines. His *Plow* book never had an original manuscript except the typed copy, since it was written on poplar leaves that crumpled and tobacco sacks he later threw away. There were only six original poems from *Plow*. These were pasted in one of his scrapbooks.

From where he stood beside his mother and father by the well, if he could have looked straight through the house he could have seen where *Plow* had its beginning. It was down at the foot of the hill by a spring from which they had carried water before this well was dug in the back yard. It was an ancient spring—a well they had found there, one already walled with rocks and all they did was clean from it the accumulated sediment which had filled it to the top. Two houses had stood on this saddle between two hills before Mick purchased his fifty acres and Shan and his Grandpa Shelton had built the house.

It was at this spring where his mother and one of his sisters gathered their wash and washed clothes, sheets, and quilts, and hung the wash on clotheslines down there. It saved packing water up the hill in big buckets. It wasn't a burden either to carry dry soiled wash down the hill and carry it both clean and dry back up the hill.

It was here while Shan's mother was washing clothes that he came in from working in the field and unharnessed the mule and let him go free in the pasture. Shan had finished plowing a field of corn. It was midafternoon. His father was away working on the railway section. His brother and youngest sister were away at Plum Grove School. Shan walked down where his mother was alone doing a wash of clothes. Just Shan and his mother were at home. His mother was washing clothes under the shade of the tall poplar that shaded the spring. There were three infant poplars with good shade for Shan, for a July sun was beaming down. There was a wooden sled, pulled by mules, beside the three poplars.

Shan sat on the sled and began to write on the inner and outer section of a tobacco sack. People, places and things were coming out of his head. His mother didn't speak to him. She left her son alone. She had always had faith in her children. She believed that each one would "make a mark in life." Right here under the poplar shade with pencil first and then stick and poplar leaves was the beginning of *Plow*. Right here, on a spot soon to be forgotten, where the three young poplars grew skyward and the sled rotted away. Here where the wind listeth now was the birth of *Plow*. From Shan's head came places and things from America, Egypt, and the Middle East and Japan. Shan's head-born children from *Plow* had reached many countries. They had gone to places he had never seen. *Plow* was legitimate and a success. *Harvest* was illegitimate and vanity. This was the beginning of the word. But *Harvest* would not die. An old copy was found later and the book reprinted. Shan didn't know whether to be glad or sorry.

Time stood still here where the winds blew over the old pasture fields and through the woods. Shan rejoiced to hear the singing winds up here. In the days when he was young and they didn't have music in his home, for not a member of his family had had any musical talents, Shan heard his music in the winds. Up here where he had spent nineteen years from boyhood to marriage, up here where he had written so much he wondered if the winds hadn't been his inspiration. He loved to hear their sounds; his face and body loved to feel what his eyes had always tried to see. Winds blowing then and now, winds, winds. Winds!

Winds blew but they didn't ruffle his mother's charcoal-black straight hair, for the bun on the back of her head was tightly pinned down with combs. Shan rolled the windlass and let the bucket down ten feet to water.

"Our neighbor and friend, Old Ugly Bird Skinner, the water witch, found a vein with his peach tree fork that never went dry," Mick said. "Twenty-two feet deep, ten feet down to the water. There is twelve feet of water in that well."

"Yes, Old Ugly Bird has come from my head three times," Shan told Mick as he lowered the bucket down into the water. "I passed by his house this morning and I didn't see anyone there."

"Time runs together, Shan," his mother reminded him. "There is no morning, noon or night."

"Remember, Shan, how I liked my watch," Mick said. "It stood railroad inspection. It never lost a minute in a year. Remember I wound my watch and hung it on a nail in my room in there. I knew I was making that walk through The Gate and I wouldn't need my good watch anymore. Seconds, minutes, hours, days, weeks, months, years are one! Time is not to be divided and paralleled like land. Time is invisible and eternal."

Shan wound the windlass lifting the full bucket of cold water straight up the well. The windlass which he turned with ease did the lifting when he wound the bucket up to where he could reach it. He set the bucket on the platform inside the well box which his father had made.

"It's pretty water," Shan said.

There was a gourd dipper hanging by the string through the handle onto a nail. One reason why the Powderjays had always raised gourds was to use them for dippers. They raised gourds to use to drink water from a bucket or a spring. Water had always tasted better when from a gourd. And they had used gourds to dip loose salt from a barrel.

But the water up to the rim of the well bucket was making movement after the lift up from the well. It didn't spill over though. Shan didn't drink of the water after he had drawn it up. His mother didn't drink of the water. She looked onto the water in the well bucket and she smiled, pleasantly. Shan had never seen her in a more pleasant mood. His mother had never been pleased as much as she had been moody and sad.

His father had always been happier more than he had been moody and sad. He had always been happy when he had someone to be happy with him. His mother had not always been happy with him. But she was happy with him now. Shan's father only looked at the water. He didn't drink either. He looked at the water and fondled the long handle of the gourd dipper. He was in a playful mood. His face was almost the color of new ground dirt. His big blue eyes were full of mischief.

"Shan, why did you draw this water when we don't want a drink?" Mick said.

"I don't know. Maybe it's because I've drawn so much water from this well! Maybe, because it is water that comes up from our good earth. Maybe it's the water of life."

There was the log house, four rooms. Attached alongside was a large lean-to, and this sprawling house was weather-boarded and painted white.

"My father's and your hands, Shan, put that house there," his mother said. "The wear and tear it had. That house has been lived in."

"Not much rock left," Mick said. "Old Dad used up all the rock here!"

There was a small portion of the big rock that was surrounded and shaded once upon a time by tall hickories. Here the hunters came and one would climb upon this rock, sit in silence until a squirrel came to one of the hickories to gather nuts, then he shot the squirrel. When Mick Powderjay bought this farm, "Old Dad" as he called Shan's grandfather, his wife's father, and Shan sawed down the tall hickories, scored and hewed them for house logs, barn logs and logs for a smokehouse. The smokehouse was still standing right before them.

"Old Dad" split the giant rock with wedges. He found, so he said, seams in the rock. He scored the sides and shaped the pieces into square ones with which he made the chimneys up through the center of the house. He laid the house foundation with these rocks. He made a cellar with them. All of this had been done on less than an acre of ground. The tall hickories, the big rock and the squirrels were gone from where the wind blew over now. Powder-jays had raised potatoes on this land and his mother had pastured her cows here.

The color of the April wind had been the same. It was not the color of light green, the early arbutus leaf or the percoon leaf that sprang so suddenly in early April. The April air which Shan, his mother and father felt against their faces was the color of the Right Fork of Academy Branch waters, waters lilting and singing over gravels and kissed by ferns. This was the way the wind was. Shan loved its color. He rejoiced to be in it—to be alive and to be with his parents who were in a happy, homecoming mood. Shan rejoiced to see them so happy together, so well-dressed for no particular reason unless it was they were meeting with Shan again after all these years.

Shan was well-dressed, too, to be with his parents. He was dressed in clothes he liked. His clothes fit his body well. He and his parents had dressed this way when they used to walk over the path the way Shan had just come to Riverton. They went to Greenwood walking over this path on Saturdays and on holidays, Fourth of July and Labor Day.

"My son, I'm so pleased with you," his mother said. "I always wanted someone to look at you and say when you walked down a Greenwood street 'There goes Mollie Shelton's son.' And that did come to pass."

"We're proud of all of our children, Mollie," Mick said.

"It would be strange for Jean and me to speak of all of our children," Shan said. "We can only speak of our one, Janet!"

Shan's mother laughed loudly.

"You can speak of many children," she told him. "You are the father of many children!"

"Only one child by one woman!"

"One child of the flesh, Shan, but you are the father of many head children."

"Oh, I see what you mean! I left some wild head children up at Kingston Hospital! I never saw such fight as there was among them. I got away and I'm here. They were head children, all right. They were very undesirable head children."

"We have blood-and-flesh undesirable children, but if they belong to us we love them just the same—that is, if the mother is a real mother and the father is a real father. If they don't love them, who will? They need love! But love is not the greatest word in the language. Faith is the greatest word."

There didn't seem to be any time. If there were time there wasn't any way to measure it. Shan could always measure time in any of the four seasons—spring, summer, autumn, winter—by the sun in the sky. But there wasn't any sun. There was the clear, clean water-over-gravel blue April wind which they were in and of which they were a part. It was a beautiful April. It was a beautiful wind. It was a beautiful world. There had never been anything like this.

Shan, with his parents now, was in a rejoicing mood! He was as happy as they. He felt as high as the sky above the earth was high. He didn't drink the beautiful water of life from the well in their great earth, and neither had his parents. They hadn't desired the water. They had just wanted to draw it from their good earth and to see it. They were the living earth, the water and the wind.

"Shan, we're going to have to leave you," his father said.

"You know, Shan, you've got to meet the train."

"No, Mom, I didn't know it!"

"You must go meet Huey the Engineer's train at Three Mile. They will be there! You will see them!"

"We will not be there," his father said. "But, we will see you later. We have old friends to see!"

"It's been so good to see you, Shan!"

"So good to see you, Mom!"

His hand clasped his mother's warm hand.

"So good to see you, Dad!"

"Yes, it has been a good meeting. Remember when we planned to raise a garden together and you got down bedfast! You had your first one! And I wound up my watch, hung it on a nail in my room and told daughter Julia and son-in-law Whitie I was going on a long journey. So we didn't get to raise the garden. Be a good boy until we meet again."

"I will, Dad! Goodby, Mom!"

They departed suddenly around the house as if they were trying to hide their path of departure. Now, together, getting along so well—each in a mood of happiness, Shan didn't want to follow or disturb them. He thought they might have other places on the farm or in the house they wanted to see. Far be it from him to disturb two of the greatest people he had ever known in his world.

No one, not even his mother could ever tell him and make him believe that flesh-and-blood children, begotten by a father and born from the womb of the mother were not better and greater than children born from the human head—his head.

But children born from the head could be around. They could be created and told about on paper and they could live forever among the flesh-and-blood people who lived much shorter lives. Head people could be mean, indifferent, good, beautiful! They could be everything. Born of the head, they could be shaped and made aware. They could be something. They could be everything. They could be nothing.

The head people could be known for generations to come, although they had never been flesh and blood, to walk upon this earth. They had never eaten food, drunk water, loved and reproduced. They were make-believe but they were here as sure as there were dirt, streams, trees, stones, mountains and skies! Head people!

Shan walked away from the house out to the Sand Gap. Here was where the old narrow road went through a sand-stone rock rim that capped a not-too-high hill. He was familiar with this road, although he had not walked over it for years, instead he drove a car to go places. And, too, with too much walking he got leg cramps. It was no longer a pleasure for him to walk—not like it had been in the younger years of his life. Now it was a pleasure again for him to walk full stride, facing the wind, breathing on purpose or unconsciously. He could do either way. But, the air was so clean and fresh he preferred the breathing.

It was great to see Uncle Mel Shelton's land again, where Uncle Mel had raised the good apples for cider. Uncle Mel had a cider press and he made gallons of cider for ten cents a gallon. He raised the finest peaches upon the hill above where Shan was walking now. Shan knew when the peaches ripened and went to the orchard where he had eaten his fill. That was when Shan was from twelve to fourteen and his father and mother rented Uncle Mel's house. That was the fifth and last house, his mother and father rented before his father bought the fifty acres and Shan and his grandfather Shelton built the house. No wonder he had a tryst with his parents there! That was the place upon this earth most dear to them. They were a part of it and it was a part of them.

Here tall poplars grew along the little stream. These were not here when he had last walked along this path. He wanted to see the old strawberry shed, which was a roof set over four posts. These posts were on sills and the sills were on large stones. Strawberries had been raised on this steep hill. They had been carried down and put under this roof to protect them from rain until they could be hauled. All this had happened before Shan was born.

Here was the old shed all right. He stepped upon the sill and looked up through the holes in the board roof. The roof needed to be repaired. The little stream trickled down by the shed.

Shan had known this was called the strawberry shed and he had played here as a boy, from the first time he could remember. Down the valley another quarter mile was the house where he had lived until he was nine. When he moved to *this* house as a child, maybe the first and longest journey he had ever walked was from this house, his home, to the strawberry shed with his mother who went to milk the cow every morning and late afternoon. When he grew to be six years old he remembered going over to the pasture and finding the cow for his mother and bringing her down to the strawberry shed to be milked. Shan was having long-ago and far-distant memories now as he stood on the sill, rocking on his tiptoes and feeling his great physical strength. He liked the April wind on his face. It was so cool and good to breathe too.

Out there was the old gate. He remembered how he and his Cousin Penny Shelton, Uncle Mel's boy, had swung on the gate until they had broken a hinge. Uncle Mel threatened to switch Penny and his father had threatened to switch him. But this never happened. Mick Powderjay never switched or spanked one of his children in his life. Shan's mother had done these "honors" when she deemed them necessary. She was the disciplinarian and the dry Baptist.

There was the grove of wild plums near the gate. Here was where Shan and his sister and Shelton cousins used to come to get ripe wild plums in their season. Now the plum trees interwove and barren branches switched in the wind.

Shan couldn't linger too long here. He had to be on

his way. He had to meet the train. He would soon be seeing Huey the Engineer. Good Old Huey! It would be great to see him and his train again.

And he had to see the house where he had lived when he was a boy and played with his brother who departed this life when he was five and Shan was seven. He had left Shan, lonely and without a playmate but another brother and a sister had been born in this house!

Walking down the narrow valley along the twisting foot path that followed a winding stream, he came to the house. The place was silent but here was the well in the back yard from which he had drawn water. Here was the old gnarled white oak in the back yard, a tree dying at the top, where their chickens used to roost. Shan had memories of this place! He had memories of his brother John who had been permitted such a brief stay upon this wonderful and beautiful earth.

His brother, born in this house, was never ten miles away from it in his lifetime. He had lived and had died here. This was the only place he had ever known. Shan and his oldest sister, Sallie, were the only two left in this world who could remember his looks. There was never a picture made of him. Yes, here the wind listeth when he had gone.

Shan's mother couldn't bear to see the last place where he and his brother John had played. They had stuck sticks in the ground for telephone poles. From a ball of white twine they had unraveled a "wire" from stick to stick. On each end they had their twine put there through the hole in a tin can. The thread was knotted so it could slip out. Shan and his brother John pretended they were talking over a telephone to each other as they had seen telegraph operators do at the Riverton Railway Station. Standing here brought back hundreds of memories to Shan. His parents had told him they found babies in the ground. They told him they had found him and John in the ground over on the bluff across the stream from the house.

After John's death, Shan had crossed the stream and had dug holes all over the bluff hunting for another brother. He dug until his mother, who was crying, stopped him. Here he stood now remembering his childhood innocence and playing with his brother.

Shan had to meet the train! He didn't know the time. There was no sun in the sky. He couldn't tell time by the sun. He didn't have his watch. His mother, before she left, had told him to meet the train! Why meet the train? There had to be a reason or his mother wouldn't have told him! If no other reason, seeing the train would be great! He'd get to see the train on which he had taken his first ride. And he would get to see Huey the Engineer again! How often he had gone to this station when he was six and older and waited for the train to come and stop so he could see Huey the Engineer sitting up there in his engine. He had wanted to grow up and be like Huey, be an engineer and drive an engine big enough to pull four cars, two of freight, one for mail, one a passenger coach, up the grades, puffing, huffing, and pulling hard through the tunnels under the hills and across the bridges that spanned the rivers.

It was good walking now down the road to the intersection of the Valley Road. This road was the same as it had always been when Shan, his sisters and brother had walked this way. It was too cool for the multi-colored butterflies to be on the rocks where valley stream crossed the road. The salt-barrel–sized sycamore, sixty feet tall, was barren—iron tracery without bud and leaf up in the April wind. When this tree, loved by everyone who lived in the Valley, was leafed, it shaded a deep hole of water where the road crossed over the stream. Butterflies alighted here on the loose stones that stuck above the rippling light-blue water. Here the butterflies liked to come to sit on the loose rocks and drink. Here mule teams pulling heavy loads of crossties or coal stopped to drink. Shan remembered all as he leaped over the stream. He had leaped this stream before. He didn't want to mess up his good shoeshine. He had thoughts of this tree where the stream crossed the road when he had played with his brother and sisters here. He remembered how they counted the butterflies on the rocks. Shan didn't have time to stop now. He had to meet the train. He was about one mile away from Three Mile Station.

Next he reached peddler's well where the road parted. The road over which he had walked with Sheltons, Howards and Fletchers made a right angle. The old Valley Road went under the long branches of a white oak tree forty feet tall with a gnarled short body about six feet in diameter and twenty feet in circumference. Shan didn't have time to estimate the circumference of its spreading boughs which were without bud and leaf. When leafed in spring and summer its shade had been larger than his father's and mother's four-room house. It was under the shadow of this tree that hundreds of people, walking, riding horseback, in buggies, surreys, hug-me-tights and automobiles in the past had stopped, sat under this white oak's shade on the grass or the giant braceroots of the tree extended above the ground in an entanglement that looked like knots of giant snakes piled together for warmth when they had come too soon into spring from hibernation.

Snakes being cold blooded could hibernate. Long sleep had kept them on this magnificent earth longer than any living creature. Shan was ever conscious of this. He remembered that, as a boy, he thought it would be great to see the gnarled braceroots around this tree turn to giant snakes and start crawling away with people sitting on them, fanning themselves with leaf-fans and having fun and a friendly visit. Would all ten, twenty, sometimes thirty people gathered here, sitting on these roots in the shade jump to their feet and start running? Would the women be screaming? So many people were afraid of snakes. Women even thought the beautiful little green snakes that lived on bugs and insects, were deadly poisonous. Shan had seen his mother pick up the little green snakes and fondle them in her hands.

Trees could impress Shan so much! Trees were living things that came out of the earth. Trees, like people, had personalities. Not any tree, with or without a personality, growing with roots in the earth was a nonentity. Shan's species was the same. Not any person born upon this earth with or without a talent or personality was a nonentity. Shan believed each human life, without any attachments or adverbs to modify him or her, was important.

Shan was always troubled by what Old Opp Akers had said: "All things that grow upon this earth was put here for a purpose. Sooner or later we'll find out what each one's purpose is." Now, Old Opp, the crazy old cuss that people took

him to be, was born in Shan's head. He was not blood and
flesh like Jean and his Janet. Old Opp belonged to Shan
for he had created him. He wasn't one of those monsters he
had left fighting back in Kingston Hospital. Monsters he
hadn't, didn't want to put down on paper. Old Opp was a
spiritual man. He certainly was one of the spirit. He had
been a spirit walking, talking, living upon Laurel Ridge.
Now he had gone to many places. People who knew Opp
believed everything was put on earth by its Creator for a
purpose.

Across from the white oak in the angle of the road, the
old well box around peddler's well was about to fall. Shan
owned this land now. He'd have Bud, so he thought, haul
rocks to fill the well. He didn't know whether it was a myth
or not that a peddler long ago had been robbed and thrown
into this well. Shan didn't know whether there were any
bones there. He'd never had it cleaned out. He had tried to
get men smaller than he to go down to see if there were
bones and a peddler's pack. Everybody knew the reputation
of this well and no one would go down into it. Shan would
have done this himself but he was too broad across his
shoulders. He could not squeeze into the circular rock wall
and bend over in this well. In his and Jean's front yard was
a well he had gone down into to clean for his father who
let him down in a well bucket when he was nine, ten,
eleven years old. One hundred fifty years ago they dug
wells for smaller people.

Who was in peddler's well? Shan had always wondered.
Why was it an untouchable? Funny, it didn't produce a
water that quenched thirst even if it were full to the surface
at all times in all seasons. It was here, Shan's Uncle Mel,

who feared not man or devil, declared when he walked past this well before daylight on his way to dig coal that something in white flew by him and snuffed out the flame on his carbide lamp attached to his bankcap. This was the light he used in the mine by which he could see to dig. Uncle Mel was an earth man. He was like a mole that liked to go under the ground to dig, dig, dig! He wasn't like Old Opp Akers, a man of the spirit. Uncle Mel was a big 225 pounder, a muscular man, afraid of the spirits, who found it more interesting to lay in the shade and read *Rise and Fall of the Roman Empire* and let his corn go unplowed and the crabgrass grow and choke it to spindly stems. Passing peddler's well before dawn, he always feared. He had seen many strange lights flashing, then instantly disappear.

What in the world—why in the world—did he have such thoughts about landmarks no one ever noticed anymore! Why was he thinking about them when he had a date with destiny? He had to meet Huey's train. Well, he was just about there. He had reached the artesian spring beside the road where the water jumped up a foot high. It came straight up from the ground! When he, his sisters and brother used to walk this way returning from Plum Grove with Sheltons, Howards and Fletchers, they used their drinking cups to catch this clean, clear, cold blue water up from the deep earth to quench their thirst. Shan wasn't thirsty for water. He didn't even want to taste it. He wasn't hungry for food either. He didn't think about food. What he wanted to do and would do was to meet the train at Three Mile.

Somewhere over the low hill and down the Eastern Kentucky tracks he thought he heard the sound of Huey's

whistle. There were only two trains on the "E.K." They
were Numbers One and Two. The railway was thirty-six
miles long. Huey pulled Number One. Huey's One left
Riverton at seven each morning. Malcolm Partlow's Number Two left Watsonville on the other end of the line at
seven. Both engineers left North and South Terminals at
the same time. They met midway at Goodlettsville. The
first train to arrive laid over on a switch to let the other train
pass. Each train pulled four cars: passenger, mail car, two
freight cars. Shan knew, for this was the first train he had
ever ridden when he was six and his sister nine.

Shan's father Mick took his son Shan and his daughter
Sallie to Three Mile Station where he had flagged Huey
with a piece of burning newspaper. Mick knew Huey and
greeted him with a warm "good morning." Then he said to
Conductor Hill McVey, "Hill, see my daughter and son
get off at Wellhope. It's a long journey for two children going to see their uncle and aunt and play with their cousins."
This was exactly as it had been.

Why was he meeting the train now?

When either of Shan's parents, Mollie Shelton Powderjay or Mick Powderjay, ever told him anything he
should do he had better do it.

He was taking big strides now, turning across and down
the hill to the flag station, Three Mile. It was just as he had
been told. He heard the train coming. He had heard this
same sound before when he was six. He remembered his
father saying "Old Huey is straining every nerve in his
little engine up the Dials Curve." It was upgrade and a
curve too. And there was the deep Bates Cut Huey's train

had to come through. The train was always almost to the station before one could see it.

Shan saw the black clouds of coal smoke billowing in clouds and spirals above the Bates Cut. He heard Huey's engine huffing and puffing and straining every nerve—black clouds, clouds—and more clouds, spiraling up and up into the blue April sky! It had to be morning but due to the strangeness of the atmosphere and no sun and no watch, Shan couldn't tell. He knew this had to be the morning train.

Shan had reached the station after a long and thoughtful journey. His legs, after much walking, were in fine fettle. He was an athlete again. His heart was like it was the day Doctor Vinnins gave him a physical checkup in Toniron, Ohio. Doctor Vinnins had said: "I wish I had your heart." Seven days later Shan had had his first massive attack. That one had almost taken his life and put him to bed for eleven months. It wasn't that way now. He didn't have to take N.G.'s when he walked briskly up and down hills the way his road ran from Riverton to Three Mile. There hadn't been any evening preceding the night when he had taken two thirds Scotch, one third branch water with a little ice to make it cool so he could drink the stuff—stuff that brought him down from a dream-world where his thoughts soared, thoughts over which he had no control.

Scotch slowed his thoughts, rested his mind, took him out of his world, made him sleepy. This had been the drink's intended purpose, something people who knew the situation, including Shan's oldest sister Sallie, couldn't understand. It was something their Baptist mother would have never tolerated. He had just been with her and maybe she knew now Shan didn't have to have his evening drink of Scotch and branch water any more before he went to bed. Let Scotch be dope or narcotic. Let nitroglycerine be the same! He didn't have to have either. He figured one day in the twenty-three years since his first attack he had taken 175,295 pills. He was happy to be set free of all medicines. He was glad to be an athlete again with the near-perfect body he had once had and he had dreamed so often of having again, lying on his own or a hospital bed—but he would awaken to sorrow that this was only a dream and not true. He wasn't dreaming now. He was very much alive, and as well and happy as he had ever been in his life.

The nose of Number One came around and out of the curve. Huey blew a long and two shorts. This was the way it was as long as Shan could remember. Huey didn't have to be flagged as his father Mick had flagged him so many times here. Shan stood back from the flag station. There was a building here. The road from the valley crossed the tracks here. There was a house up on the top of a little hill overlooking the station. The Brauns lived here. Their family, father, mother and six children used to walk out into the yard and look down each morning, wave or speak to Huey. So many people asked him the time of day, set their watches and clocks by his perfect time piece, his "railroad" watch, same as Mick Powderjay had carried a lifetime, wound his watch, hung it on a nail in his room, to keep time forever before he departed to walk through The Gate from one world to another.

Huey pulled his engine up slowly now to where the engine was beyond the road that crossed over. But there was no one out in Braun's house. There was no one out on the porch when Huey blew a long and two shorts to see who got off or on the train. There wasn't a person, animal or automobile on the road, Huey's train didn't block person or persons walking or riding on the highway.

Huey was up there in his engine all right. He wore his pin-striped cap with a jumper to match with a red bandanna as big as a shawl around his neck. He was the man when Shan was six he wanted to grow up and be like—wear railroad clothes, a red bandanna and have his hand on the throttle, looking out and down over the houses, fields, hills, valleys, rivers and towns as his engine burned the rails—steel against steel—bumpety-bump, bang, bang, bang—a cowcatcher that kept the ragweeds cut down that grew between the crossties and the bright-topped rails! What a life this would be, Shan used to think as he looked at little Huey the Engineer, all 120 pounds of man, with his long hair flying with the wind, and his head out of the cab window as he looked at the track ahead over which his train had to pass.

Shan, standing back from the train, saw something he couldn't believe! Huey was pulling four passenger coaches. The mail car and two freight cars weren't in his train. The coaches were loaded with people and some of them were very strange looking. He could see them from his side of the train through the windows. He could see them rising from their seats without order. They were pushing past each other to get off the train. But only those on the first coach could get off now. Passengers on three coaches had to wait for Conductor Hill to let them off. He was the good conductor who looked after his passengers. Huey was the good engineer who had pulled his train fifty years and never had a casualty. There was the Conductor Hill McVey with the blue suit and brass buttons, the blue cap with a long black bill. He was helping them off the first coach. He had placed his little footstool down for the passengers to step down on.

First woman to come down the steps was wearing a split skirt which showed her not-too-attractive legs. She wore silk stockings that gathered close to her legs and a blouse opened low in front. Her lips were spread in a broad smile showing her very white teeth. Nearly all of Shan Powderjay's head children had good teeth. Maybe this was because he, a flesh-and-blood man, had sound and beautiful teeth up until his first massive heart attack.

"Watch your step, lady," Conductor Hill said in his soft southern gentleman's voice. "I don't want anybody hurt!"

"Thank you for calling me a lady," she said. "I like that word very much. I'm not a lady. I'm Aunt Viddie Tussie. I married my Uncle. I slept with him before we were married, too. I married Uncle George."

"And here I am with my Viddie," said Uncle George. "Where you see one you see the other! Conductor Hill, let me tell you as man and wife we have traveled! We've been over most of the world and a lot of funny people have laughed at us! We've made millions laugh! You see anything funny about us?"

Shan knew how right his mother had been. She had told him to meet this train. She knew he would be in for a surprise! He had spoken to her of Jean and their only child, flesh-and-blood daughter Janet. She had reminded him of his head children! Huey the Engineer, his train, the tracks, and Conductor Hill McVey, Shan had put on book pages. They had been born from his head. They were head children, too.

"Our whole Tussie Family is on this train," Aunt Viddie said. "We got up front in the first coach. We are the people who liked to get there first and get everything we could get. We like to dance, frolic and love. We are like the flesh-and-blood people everywhere in this world that we have been."

"May I ask you, Mrs. Tussie, why I have so many passengers on our train?"

"Our father is dead," Aunt Viddie replied. "Shan Powderjay created us! He is our father. We are going to his funeral!"

"It's only natural children go to their father's funeral," said Uncle George, tall and shaky.

His white hair tousled by the young blue April wind, he said, "We are his head children!"

"To think I created them," Shan thought. "I'll be going to this funeral too! I'll be seeing what goes on! I'll see who's there!"

"Funeral services for our father will be in the Plum Grove Chapel," said the voice of the third Tussie coming down the steps. "I'm Kim Tussie. I was Viddie's legal husband killed in the war. I wasn't killed. Brother Mott knew the body sent home wasn't mine. I came home and found her married to my uncle. He wooed her with his fiddle. Too old a man for a beautiful warm flame! But it didn't matter then and it doesn't matter now since we are head people and our father, Shan Powderjay, will be laid to rest at Plum Grove beside Mick and Mollie, his flesh-and-blood parents and his small brother."

"Only the husk of what was me," Shan thought. "The real Shan Powderjay, all 225 pounds of muscle, flesh, blood and bone is alive, happy and feeling great."

Shan knew that he was seeing Huey, Conductor Hill and the train. He was watching his head children coming down the coach steps to the stool Conductor Hill had put there.

Aunt Viddie Tussie didn't wear a hobbled skirt that would contain her steps. Her split skirt allowed her legs to show almost all the way up. Shan's watching and listening to her made him wonder why he had ever created her. He couldn't believe it; he would have done it when he was younger. He wouldn't have created her in the seventieth year of his natural life. There had been a time and place for the creation of his head children. Head creation of humanity had to be all the way around like a circle. His world was round. His stars were round. The coil of the serpent was round. Even life was a circle. There was the beginning and the ending. The ending returned to the beginning.

"I'm Old Grandpa Tussie! I'm head of the Tussie Clan! And beside me is Grandma Tussie! Yes, and there is little Sid, our grandson! He took our name. Sid was a Seagraves. We're all here! All forty-six who filled the Rayburn Mansion!"

Shan didn't know all the nameless Tussies of the clan who gathered there to frolic, dance, love, eat on Aunt Viddie's pension she had received on Kim's death. This was some family getting off the train to attend his, their father's, funeral.

"We've been places farther away than the days when I cut timber in Michigan," Grandpa said. "All over South and Central America. All over Europe—even as far away as Australia. We've been places our father has never been! People have seen us who have never seen him!"

Aunt Viddie, Uncle George, Grandpa and Grandma, Uncle Kim, Uncle Mott and little Sid, with other unknowns of the Tussie Clan, left the train, walking up the railroad track. Route 1 was parallel to the E.K. Railway. The Tussies preferred walking up the tracks and stepping on the crossties. Uncle George walked on one rail to show his youth and agility while Aunt Viddie walked on the other. Uncle George and Viddie held hands across the tracks.

"Brother George, if you can do that we can do it too," Shan heard old Grandpa say.

Then, Grandpa and Grandma Tussie got up on the rails and walked and held hands across the tracks. They walked better on their dancing feet than Uncle George and Aunt Viddie. All the Tussies had dancing feet. Uncle Mott and Uncle Kim followed with Sid at their heels stepping on the crossties. Some clan of Tussies going up the rails and stepping on the ties!

"I'm glad, Huey, we've got that awful crowd out of the car," Conductor Hill called up to Huey. "Now, will you pull the train up for the next coach?"

Carefully, Huey the Engineer pulled Number One, barely inching it the length of a coach. The second loaded coach was up where the first one was. The coach steps were straight down to Conductor Hill's footstool.

"Huey, this coach has the Plow people," Shan heard Conductor Hill say.

Shan was still standing back a few feet from the train where he could see his created children. They were not sired by male and born of woman as he had been. He could see them, for he had created them not in his image but many images. He could see them but they could not see him. If they could have seen their father they would not have recognized him.

Shan knew the first of the Plow people to step down. She was Georgia Greene, among the crowd a woman giant who chewed tobacco, drank kerosene. Conductor Hill backed away from her.

He'd not forget Katherine Darter, who followed after Dick Hailey. Shan remembered their shotgun wedding, how Katherine's Pappie marched Dick in front of a gun and made him marry Katherine. Dick had gone too far with his daughter.

Old Happy Jack followed after, shaking all over with laughter. He was one who made the people happy. Shan was recognizing his children all right.

Beautiful Sadie Williams with her fatherless Little Leonard with her, was next. Her Big Leonard had fled to the west when he got her pregnant and they were not wed.

Then came queenly and attractive Quadroon Mott. She was like the late March and early April blossom of trailing arbutus and percoon.

He thought the next down was Lief McCowan, who

hadn't followed the pursuits of his fighting kin and learned it was better to be above the ground than under it.

No question about old beardy-faced Bill Powers, chew of tobacco, big as a duck's egg, behind his jaw and a basket on his arm.

Don Colley, who liked whiskey and women, and Charles Stafford who liked to sit by the stream and watch October leaves go drifting by came down the steps together.

Then, Jet Fillson and her seven daughters, Young Jet, Florine, Mand, Margaret, Billy Jo, Lucy and Mary Ann. Mother and daughters all beautiful. They had followed their mother's way of life. They were unwed, but had birthed children. Shan wondered why he had created such beautiful women, made them so loose in their morals, when he had tried so hard to be a moral man himself.

Old Charlie Splean, who cursed and hated the law all his life, followed the mother and seven daughters. Then Conductor Hill had to help Sib and Tom Kales, their heads as white as snowballs, down the steps. Arm in arm, these old people were trying to help each other.

"The fire in us is out," Tom told Conductor Hill.

Fred Sowards, who remembered the sound of the guns at Verdun, Aisne, Metz and Belleau Wood, followed.

Shan had filled Walter Blair with song, when he created him, and he came down the steps singing.

A woman followed him. Shan wasn't sure but she could have been Amanda Church. These Plow people were something else. The men were husky and the women attractive and beautiful. Among them, man desired woman and woman desired man. They were much-alive, red-blooded Americans all right! They were people of the earth.

Wade Fillson stepped down with head bowed because in his created word-life he had been jilted by his sweet Annie Lee.

Sam Rankin, an old man who stole a sixteen-year-old girl to be his bride, returned from somewhere in the west "for our father's funeral."

Bert Skaggs, who worked like hell to feed his family from land but was robbed by "pinhookers," returned for the funeral. He was a husky earth man who followed the plow.

Pretty and big-bosomed Moll Weston, who beat up Fannie Spry over her husband Bill, came down the steps without Bill. Shan had always wondered why Bill would ever want to leave her for any other woman.

Lance Holt, a bachelor who had grieved all of his life because he let Jenny Holt marry Albert Payne, came down the steps.

There was Loretta Aimes, a Plow woman, so physically attractive she had caused men to lust. She could not help from being beautiful. Could what she had done be called sin?

Leonard Kerry, who had wronged Louella and let her bear his bastard child, lived to regret this all his life. There was Harvey Hillman, who loved Polly Jones but lost her. Mary Tongs and her John who worked away from home in the coal mines and left her lonely at home. Little Millard Artis came down the steps. He had lived in a cabin alone on Seaton Hill.

Shan recognized Tim Long, who was serving in the pen for making moonshine whiskey. He was allowed out for his father's funeral. There was Kim Sperry, a hard-working share-cropper who had paid half of all he grew to the land-owners. There was Milton Sloan, who hid his past among the hills. Only Milton knew what his past had been.

There was Warren Winslow, whose health had been better since he moved to a small farm among the hills where he could hear the wind in the leaves and sit on a mossy stone by the valley stream and hear the waters flow.

There was No Coward Charlie Thombs, who was always looking for a fight. There was Lemuel Potter and his wife, who were children of the night because they couldn't read or write. They worked to send their children to school so life would be different for them.

Shan counted five people—three men and two women—he didn't recognize.

Then, Jud and Min Moore and their nine daughters appeared. Jud and Min had been sent to the pen for making moonshine back in the depression years. Their nine unwed daughters had slept with different men while their parents were away in the pen.

Now, the long sleepers arose from their ancient beds and passed Conductor Hill in single file. Tish Meadows, William Thomas, silly Sue Pitts, Bunion Maddox, Laura Maddox, Ephraim Boone, Tobias Holbrook, Press Hylton, Winston Campbell, Elizabeth Graves, Ina Callihan, Maud Clements, Boyd Steel and Virginia Barr. There was Katherine Dunn, her small son Willis, her daughter Grace. Ferris Hare begot her daughter; Martin Hill begot her son. She lived with Cauldwell Spence and he did not get her a son or daughter. She was never married to anyone.

"Some crowd of people going to Shan Powderjay's

funeral," Conductor Hill told Huey. "Look at the Plow people walking up that railroad track. Someone told me these Plow people had come from Japan."

Shan knew they had come from all over America, Egypt and Japan.

"Move the next coach up, Huey!"

When Conductor Hill opened the door of the third car Shan got the surprise of his lifetime. He couldn't believe what he was seeing.

First down the steps was Old Glory Gardner from Blakesburg. He wasn't carrying an American flag and giving a patriotic speech but he was in a hurry.

"Oh, oh, trouble coming," thought Shan, remembering how violently the real-life people of the town had reacted when the book was published.

Then there was old Judge Whittlecomb with the finest pair of legs in Kentucky, who used to take his walks on the Blakesburg streets and play his games of solitaire at the Winston Boarding House. He was still on that pair of fine long legs walking down the steps.

There was Liam Winston, his mother, Aunt Effie, best cook in Blakesburg, and there was Liam's brother Booten. Liam and his brother Booten had fought with knives. Shan had created these human monsters and they were now going to his funeral. They were like the monsters he had created at Kingston Hospital whom Doctor McAilster had to shoot with a needle.

Along came Pat Greenough and Aliss Denwiddie, last scions of two arch-rival political parties, who had grown up, loved each other and married. People knew the world was coming to an end. What did it matter then when and if rival political parties were joined?

Positive the end of the world had come in Blakesburg was Judge Ollie, running down the steps, who confessed in a time of the world's ending to his illegitimate son.

Rufus Litteral, who didn't know his father was Bolmer Tussie, and Charlie Allbright came running down the coach steps. They nearly knocked Conductor Hill over. They were in a hurry to get to the funeral.

There was Attorney Joe Oliver. He had to keep his curtains drawn for fear of people he had prosecuted shooting through his windows.

Old Muff Henderson, the two-stepper, who had danced the two-step so long he walked this way, two-stepped down the coach steps. Shan had always been proud of Old Muff—proud he had created him. He had outlasted three wives who couldn't keep up with his two-stepping. His last and fourth wife, a red-neck girl, stuck with him although she weakened before the end. These crazy people were Shan's head children.

As Shan watched these Glory children coming from the third coach, he had to think about what had happened to him in Blakesburg when his Glory book was born. Only two copies sold in Blakesburg. He was threatened in unsigned letters. When he visited the town to buy supplies to take back to his valley home, he carried a revolver. The letters he received were violent ones. He read them upside down and threw them in his waste paper basket.

His thirty-four main Glory characters, plus minor ones and accessories, filled an E.K. coach. These head people reminded him how it had been too dangerous to portray his friends and neighbors. He learned how hostile flesh-and-blood people could be and were right up to the time Jean rushed him to the hospital. When the Glory people appeared in print, all of Blakesburg was hostile to him and Jean. Shan had thought they, with their young daughter, Janet, only four, would have to move away. Jean and Shan decided to stay for this land, much loved, was theirs, too. They went to church where no one would attack them. Very unpopular, they continued to live in the valley and go to church in Blakesburg. They never retreated, even when their daughter was attacked as a small girl in the city schools. Maybe it was too bad Shan Powderjay had ever created the very warm and humorous Glory people. But here they were alive and getting off this train.

Surely that was Malinda Sprouse, a big woman who washed and ironed clothes. She knew it was the aurora borealis over Blakesburg and the world wasn't coming to an end. Many people owed her for past washings and ironings so she got out and collected her bills while the time was right.

There was old Eddie Birchfield running down the steps. He had been scared by the same Northern Lights in Blakesburg where he had established the first garage. Poor old Eddie, who "didn't drink and smoke," but how he could love. He was a pioneer in Blakesburg in mechanical arts.

There was Ronnie Roundtree, a red-neck who fought for General MacArthur but said his wife didn't have any more appeal for him than a gate post.

Next to the last Glory people to come from the coach was Jad Hix. He warned the people in front of the Winston

Boarding House this wasn't the end of time. Jad was a man who went by signs.

The thirty-sixth and last before the break of dawn was Reverend John Whetstone. Preacher John, a retired minister, told the people it was only the aurora borealis. The people wouldn't believe this gray-haired retired minister whom Shan Powderjay had created.

"Too many in that coach," Conductor Hill said. "There they go! Look at them."

Will they cause disturbances at the funeral? Shan wondered, remembering things of the past. He wasn't sure about this coach-load of his Glory children who had caused him so much trouble. They were the head people of Shan's hometown, Blakesburg. They were so different to the Tussies and the Plow people. Would they get along with them? These Glory people were a different breed of people, but let them go on and find out, Shan thought as he watched them running down the railway tracks. How could he be father to such people? Why would they be at his funeral to see him buried?

"All right, Huey, pull her up." Conductor Hill said as he signaled with his hand. "This will be the last car of this load! I'll be glad!"

Huey inched his engine up the track. When Conductor Hill motioned downward with his white gloved hands, the car came to an abrupt stop with the coach steps in line with the footstool.

When the first person walked out Shan certainly recognized her. Her platinum-blond hair was moved by the April wind. She was as fair as flesh could be—the fairest of the fair and the rarest of the rare—for Shan Powderjay had created her that way. She was a woman other women and girls had wept over. Shan had always thought she was a woman's woman, maybe the finest he had created. She was Dentsia Huntoon, one of the Melungeons of East Tennessee. She had married out of her clan.

Behind her was her husband, a timber cutter, Dave Stoneking, a broad-shouldered, husky WASP from Virginia. He'd loved Dentsia Huntoon from first sight and he married her. Her life was his life and he would defend her to the end.

"Lady, are you going to the funeral, too?" Conductor Hill asked her.

"Yes, to the funeral of my father," Dentsia replied. "Shan Powderjay is dead. He created us. He is our father."

Shan was so impressed with his daughter Dentsia that he almost went over to speak to her. She would not have known who he was because he would not have identified himself.

Next to come down the steps was a very young and active Did. He was the little city boy turned hunter. And behind him was his partner Sparkie.

Behind Sparkie and Did came Arn and Peg. Arn was Sparkie's real mother. Peg, who walked on a wooden leg was Sparkie's stepfather, a real father too, for Sparkie didn't know who his father was.

Thousands of youth all over America knew Sparkie and Did. Maybe they envied Sparkie and Did who didn't go to school. They hunted, trapped and caught a man who burned barns. Sparkie, Did, Arn and Peg had traveled, too, for people know them in Europe.

Sheriff Eric Bradley walked down the steps behind

Crooks Cornett, the man he had arrested for draft evasion who hadn't heard there was a war. When he heard the news he enlisted to fight.

A noble creation! Shan couldn't miss his Old Red Mule, whiskers and all. He tried to save mules. Red Mule had visited in twenty-six countries of the world! Old Red Mule so large and with a beard, loved animals! He loved mules. He tried to save them to the point that many tractors that were replacing them were beaten up by sledge hammers. No one knew who did it. Red Mule died in a barn eating mule feed with the eighty-six mules he was trying to save from the "glue factory," but Shan had to say fewer to make his book plausible to get it published.

Ah, Corbie, Shan's seat mate at Plum Grove! Corbie the dancer and the jew's harp player who came well dressed to the Plum Grove one-room school, better dressed than any other pupil. This was because his mother and father loved their child of the unsound mind. Shan sat by him and loved him, too. He never went beyond his primer.

Yes, Corbie was coming down the steps on his dancing feet, coming to Shan's funeral!

Old big Timmie Phelps, Shan's boyhood friend, who had a phobia about fire and was burned to death, came waddling down the steps. He went up the tracks following the others.

"All right, Huey, we've unloaded," said Conductor Hill.

This was the time for Shan to say something. He had stood in the background. He had seen Conductor Hill unload four coaches. He walked over to him.

"Can you tell me more about this funeral?" he said.

"All I can tell you is we will back Number One to

Riverton and bring it back loaded to Three Mile," said Conductor Hill, who had collected and read all of Shan's books. "They will walk the last mile to their father's funeral. Hundreds of people, maybe two thousand more, are waiting to ride on our train. We have the Destiny people. There could be five hundred of these beautiful people at Riverton waiting for us. Then we have the Story people. There could be from one to two thousand of these. I'll tell you, we have people to haul. I've never seen such a funeral."

"There are the Thread and Gallion people to bring," he added with a sigh. "Shan Powderjay has a lot of children who are coming from all over our country and the world for his funeral. Are you going?"

"Yes."

"You had better get along while we back Number One to Riverton to pick up another load. I don't know how many we'll bring."

Shan's Destiny and Story sons and daughters would, maybe, number two or three thousand. How could Huey and Conductor Hill bring all these to Three Mile on his little train?

Shan realized it was time for him to be on his way to Plum Grove. He had been at Three Mile too long. He had watched Conductor Hill unload his children, handling them with his white gloves.

"Will you make connections with Malcolm Partlow at Goodlettsville at noon?" Shan asked.

"No, we can't," Conductor Hill said. "We may have to meet with him at Riverton. We have so many of Shan Powderjay's children to haul to Three Mile for his funeral at Plum Grove."

"Do you know the man Shan Powderjay?"

"No! No one exactly knows this man. He is as legendary as the Melungeons! Who knows about them? Where they are from and where they are going? No one really knows Shan Powderjay or has ever known him. All we know is the man is dead. We know all these people are going to his funeral. I've never seen so many who claim to be his children!"

Huey's whistle blew. Huey's Number One had to back down to Riverton to pick up more passengers.

Shan watched Huey back his train. He was up in his engine with his hand on the throttle, with wind tousling his long hair from under his pin-striped cap. He watched Huey's train back down the Bates Cut, hidden by high banks on either side. He watched the clouds of smoke rolling up from the little engine's tall stack. He didn't wait to see more of his children arrive. He started walking down the E.K. tracks stepping from one crosstie to another. He was on his way.

Shan walked behind all the hundreds who had gotten off the train and who were on their way to Plum Grove. Maybe, there would be two, three, four, or five more trainloads of children coming to his funeral. He must walk from Three Mile over the old familiar road where hundreds had gone before him.

The road from Three Mile to Plum Grove hadn't changed much since he was a boy. He had walked barefooted over it from July until October when frost compelled him to wear his first and only pair of brogan shoes. Walking up to the crossing where there was a cowcatcher on the tracks, Shan turned right. When he walked a hundred yards on this road he saw a large blacksnake sunning that reminded him of Old Ben, lying upon a bent tree. He stopped, picked up a stone and threw it at the snake. He didn't try to hit it. The snake didn't move.

As he walked on another two hundred yards, he met crawling toward him the largest blacksnake he had ever seen. He looked at the snake and the snake looked at him. He knew this snake had to be his wonderful pet, Old Jackson. Strange about two snakes. Why would they be on this road?

Where was Old Annis Bealer, who wore heavy clothes in summer to keep out heat! Had there ever been another man like him? Where were his other Plum Grove people, his head children that had gone all over the world from these Plum Grove Hills? Where were they? Shan didn't expect them here! Not among the hills where they were born. They had gone to schools all over America. Some few had gone into textbooks in foreign countries.

Yes, men, women and children from the Plum Grove Hills! Would they be at their father's funeral? He had created them, too!

Shan walked the road around to the place where Old Annis Bealer had a watering trough where people could stop and water their horses. This was a thing of the past. Automobiles passed now where those on horseback and in wagons and buggies drove by here and stopped to water their horses. Now senseless, non-loving machines stopped at gasoline pumps.

Beyond the watering place was Old Annis Bealer's big log house with the steep roof and four tall chimneys. On either side of the road were two fences. These were made of barbed wire, five strands, and the locust fence posts were set ten feet apart. These were fences Annis built to keep his livestock in their pastures. The fence rows didn't have a briar or a sprout growing in them.

From the time he was a boy until he was nineteen, Shan had seen Old Annis wearing a wool shirt and corduroy coat and pants in hot July while he was cutting out his fence rows. He believed what would keep out cold would keep out heat. He had often told Shan when he talked to him along the road that when he lay down in bed and tried to think that he could think through steel. Shan thought Old Annis must be close to him now watching every step he made. Shan knew he felt this man's presence, for this beautiful and well-kept farm had been his Heaven on earth. Shan's father, Mick, had modeled his fifty-acre farm on Annis Bealer's three hundred acres. Shan had modeled his thousand acres on Annis Bealer's and his father's.

There was no one behind Shan on the Plum Grove Road. Huey and Conductor Hill McVey hadn't had time to back Number One from Three Mile to Riverton.

Shan hurried his footsteps so he was taking almost three-foot strides, toward his motherless children ahead. They had only a father. They were loyal to him all right. They were coming to see their father buried. Shan walked alongside Annis Bealer's largest bottom where he was the first farmer in Greenwood County to raise one hundred bushels of corn per acre. Shan was in the Plum Grove School that July and August in 1916 when men came from far and near on horseback, in buggies and jalopies with cranks, over the rough and rutty roads to look at Annis Bealer's corn and ask him how he did it. This was before commercial fertilizers. Annis had used barnyard manure and leaves he had raked from his woodlands, spread these over his fields, plowed them under. Manure and leaves held moisture for the roots of corn. Annis Bealer must have been the first to use leaves for compost. Now city people who had shade trees and little gardens were doing this all over America.

How smart Old Annis had been. He couldn't read or write in German or English. But, Old Annis could "think through steel." Shan didn't remember the big corn as well as he had remembered the morning-glories vining up the tall corn stalks, after the third and last plowing and giving beauty to the world with their white, blue and pink bell-shaped blossoms. How he had walked along this dusty road barefooted as a small boy on his way to school, carrying his small lard-bucket lunch pail, having it swinging in rhythm as he walked proudly, never thinking then why he was on this earth, looking at the tall corn and morning-glory blossoms and dew drops on the corn blades that were sparkling like diamonds in the early morning sun. Now it was different. Shan was well dressed in his double-breasted blue serge suit, one he'd always liked, his white shirt, black tie tied in a perfect knot—only he could tie that kind of knot. Even his black-laced shoes were not dusty. His black wool socks that Jean had purchased for him were soft and warm on his feet. No more cold feet. Walking had helped keep his feet warm.

Right now his world was as perfect as it had ever been. As he reached the end of the cornfield on his left, the road forked. One road turned left and went down Shacklerun Valley, past the Darter and Kiel farms. This had always been called the Road to Life. The road to his right, which Shan had to take to follow his children, was the Road to

Death. It wound like a blacksnake crawling up the hill. This road went up a hill where there had once been groves of wild plum trees. Now there were none. There were only haws which were small thorny trees to which Shan and his classmates used to try to outrun each other to get there first to eat the ripe red and black fruit.

Shan looked at the haw trees on his right. There was a grove of these trees that had lasted half a century. To his left were the young pasture fields where he and his classmates used to chase the ground squirrels and coveys of quail. His old schoolhouse where he had received twenty-one months of elementary education (all he had before he entered Greenwood High School) was gone. Behind the Plum Grove schoolhouse was the Plum Grove Cemetery where Shan used to look from his window a few feet away and see a coffin carried to a freshly dug grave. There was no way he and other classmates could keep from hearing the relatives and friends crying over a lost one.

Just across the road from the schoolhouse was the Plum Grove Chapel where the funerals were preached, songs were sung, the dead viewed for the last time in their coffins. Once Shan had read: "It wasn't the cough that carried you off, but the coffin they carried you off in." This had made him laugh. He'd never forgotten these words.

Where the schoolhouse had once been was less than an acre of donated land, and that had been taken over as part of the cemetery. Here no one had ever paid for a gravesite. Here until recently community citizens dug graves free of charge. Now all lots were taken in this cemetery. Shan's father and mother, whom he had just visited with a few hours earlier at their old home were buried here. An infant brother and John, his playmate childhood brother, were buried beside his father and mother.

Now he could see the white stones behind the steel fence where his people, his friends, neighbors were taking their last long sleep. They were sleeping on this hilltop, one of the prettiest, cleanest, best-kept cemeteries in America. Not any Pennsylvania Dutch cemetery that Shan had seen had anything on the beauty and cleanliness of his Plum Grove Cemetery. It had perpetual care. It was a model rural Kentucky cemetery. Shan and his people were the helpers and supporters that had made it that way. The Plum Grove people were the best workers and planners of any people Shan had known.

Still there was such feeling among some of the flesh-and-blood people here, that they had said if Shan Powderjay were buried here they would request to be buried elsewhere. Not among their deceased kin and friends, but someplace among strangers like a cemetery in Auckland, where lots would be expensive. They wouldn't have better perpetual care in Auckland's city of the dead than they would have had at Plum Grove. Old Estelle Denton had had the talk in the presence of Shan's oldest sister, Sallie.

"If Old Shan Powderjay is buried at Plum Grove, I don't want to be buried there!"

Estelle's pioneer ancestors were buried at Plum Grove. They had donated the land one century and a half ago.

"Shan Powderjay has written stories, books, poems about a third of the people buried there," Estelle told Sallie. She tightened her lip and made an ugly face at her.

Sallie, Shan's oldest sister who read his books and was

always defending him, didn't reply to Estelle. She knew Estelle was right.

"Sallie Powderjay, if you are not aware, I'll remind you I'm not the only one who feels this way," Estelle said.

Sallie turned and walked away from her antagonist.

Shan Powderjay had two books and parts of three others on people sleeping here. He had Story people under mounds with white head markers, recording their names, dates of birth and deaths and epitaphs. He had Poetry people here. Not any author in America would be buried among a greater number of his flesh-and-blood people whom he had recorded in novel, biography, poetry, story, article than Shan Powderjay. His husk would lie among them.

Shan Powderjay, the real Shan Powderjay, was alive. He was full of life, health and energy. He was right here walking up the last steep lap of the Plum Grove Hill to where he heard voices and laughter. He could see the crowd gathered there. He could hear their voices and laughter.

When he walked up on the Plum Grove Hill, which was a low hill surrounded on three sides by valleys, he could look in all directions at the low-lying hilltops under the blue high dome of April sky. To his right was the white stone Plum Grove Chapel with a spire on the top and a cross on the front. There it was, the cross, a symbol, his symbol. He never wore a cross in his life. He didn't have to wear one for a symbol. His was implanted within him. His was invisible. The Kingdom was Within him. A cross didn't have to be worn to show who he was. His Kingdom Within him had decided everything he had done.

Yes, he was alive, so very much alive! His thinking was good. He was remembering every person, place or thing, he had ever known! What he liked most about himself was that all pain had vanished from him. He knew he would never have any more pain. Why had people upon his earth, the finest people he had ever known, had to go through The Gate because of heart attacks and long, lingering illnesses? Why had they ever had to know the agonies of cancer and the unbearable pains of heart attacks? Yes, why and why? Maybe, because it was meant to be that way.

Now, dying was different. It could be very different. Sometimes it could be with little pain. Dying could be walking through The Gate over into something rich and strange! Here he was—he had walked after he had got off Number Seven at Riverton, all the way out home, then to Three Mile Flag Station on Eastern Kentucky Railway to see Huey the Engineer and Conductor Hill unload four passenger cars filled with his children.

Right on the Plum Grove Hill his children were gathered around, standing close and some of them, like Old Grandpa Tussie and Uncle George, were very tall. They were looking at the pile of fresh dirt and a canopy, something like a tent, spread high and above the hole in the Plum Grove earth.

When Shan went through the Plum Grove Gate into his City of the Dead, a living man, he observed first the dirt that would enclose and hide forever his husk. His borrowed dust from the earth had been good and reliable. It had made him strong and handsome in his younger years. It had given him a fertile mind. His had been durable living dust from the earth that had carried him ever onward and upward as he had tried to reach the stars.

Out in front of him standing around the place where

their father would be laid was a crowd of his children. They were looking the place over and talking about how one who had created so many of them would occupy such a little portion of earth in the end, when Shan Powderjay's over-used, overworked valiant dust would be returned to his mother earth for its finality.

Of Shan Powderjay's head-born children the majority of them were never flesh-and-blood. A few of his characters had been flesh-and-blood born but Shan had rebirthed them in his head with wide variances to make them plausible to people who read about them.

There were his head-born characters who would never have a grave and headstone with a tombstone, name, dates of birth and death, and a nice epitaph with the last good words about him or her carved in granite. They were going from stone to stone reading the names, dates of birth and deaths and the epitaphs of the Plum Grove dead. There were the world's forgotten dreamers lying here.

Then, there were those like some of the Tussies who were looking at their own names, dates of births and deaths —and reading last good words carved for them in their stones.

Shan watched his children who had arrived early and who were now busily engaged checking out this Plum Grove City of the Dead.

Shan, who could not be seen by his children, was in full control of his situation. He was the master of his destiny here. He watched Old Opp Akers stand by Mick Powder-jay's stone. Old Opp had never liked Mick because Mick had contended that flower or fauna that didn't contribute something for mankind on this earth should be eliminated and not given space to grow. Old Opp contended all fauna and flora were put on earth for a purpose and if man would only wait long enough the purpose of each tree, flower, herb would be discovered.

Shan could hear people walking the winding road up the Plum Grove Hill. He walked to the Plum Grove Gate and he could see them. These were the Destiny people, Shan knew, for John and Kathleen Sutton, two beautiful people, were in front leading them! There must be three hundred and fifty people on the Plum Grove Hill road. They were walking up the hill, past Shan, who stood outside the gate.

"You ask me if there is a living God!" Shan knew his voice. Here he followed clapping his big thick hands like low claps of thunder! Shan knew he was Albert Diesel. He was a Destiny child and a child of Destiny. Shan had created this believer. He was among the crowd. He was here to see the husk of his creator planted in his good earth. He was here to see Shan's rich borrowed dust, once so much alive with blood flowing through veins like water through the waterseeps of earth, laid back to amalgamate with his mother earth. It was all earth, wind, water and spirit in the end. These were the last finalities. Not one of these could be killed. Each one was everlasting.

There was old Pat Hennessey who took life easy and lived as he pleased going through this Plum Grove Gate. It wasn't The Gate Shan first passed through, which was The Gate from Life to Life. This Plum Grove Gate was for the flesh-and-blood living to go through and visit the City of their Dead. Shan, so much alive, had followed through behind the children he had created who were not fenced by steel fences, by rivers, valleys, streams and gateways on the paths of wind. They could not be fenced. They could be invisibles on the pathways of the winds! They were imprints and implants of a fertile brain.

As the long line passed through the gate, the Plum Grove City of the Dead began to fill up. There was much talking and getting acquainted among Shan's children. Hardly any of them had met the other children except in one book or one story. Before the funeral, which would surely be at two p.m. flesh-and-blood time, was the time for them to meet and get acquainted. Each felt their relatives and friends would want to know one another.

Shan knew there was more to come when down below, near the base of the hill, at the turn of the road came another crowd. These had to be his Story people for a tall man walked in front. He was the Governor of Kentucky once. He was dressed in a tailored suit wearing a big umbrella hat.

Many of the flesh-and-blood people, walking alive upon this earth, couldn't see that this cemetery was filled with Shan Powderjay's children or know that he would be having the biggest funeral ever held at Plum Grove. This large cemetery was almost filled with his children now.

More of his children were coming up the hill. They would have to go to the Plum Grove Chapel yard. They could fill the road between the Chapel and the steel fence that enclosed the Plum Grove dead. Maybe there would be so many of Shan's head children, if all got there, many would have to stand outside the graveyard fence in the young pasture and peep through the squares in the heavy steel wire to see their father buried. Turning to see the

road again, Shan saw Old Charlie, a Story man coming up
the hill with hundreds behind him. Shan saw many a
familiar face, but he could only recall a few of their names.

He was glad now that he had created so many people.
He was glad he had stayed home among his people—people
he had known for four generations—where his songs and
stories were. He was glad he had lived his near three-score
and ten years, for fifty of which he had been begetting all
of these people in his head. Three thousand could be on
this hilltop. Huey couldn't be hauling them all on Number One with four coaches and one conductor. They could
just have walked here. They could be coming from all
roads leading toward Plum Grove. They had to take this
one road now up to the hilltop. The crowd was something
to see.

Shan could hear the talk and laughter among his children now. He knew very soon flesh-and-blood people
would be riding up the Plum Grove Hill road in their automobiles. They would be following the hearse driven by
King with Big Thomas beside him. He knew here in this
hearse would be his husk in a steel casket. It would be going
to his concrete vault in a Plum Grove grave.

It wouldn't matter about the steel casket and concrete
vault to contain his enriched resignation—the real Shan
Powderjay had gone through The Gate from one life to
another. The real Shan Powderjay was right here on this
Plum Grove Hill in the most glorious time of his life.

Faith, he knew now, was a rich substance. He knew
it had to come from within. He had always known not to
put his faith in political leaders, or in dollars which were
all right for an intended good use. He had put faith in his

good earth of which he was a part—bone, blood, flesh and
brain. He had cared for his acres more than he had his
dollars. His acres were his earth children which he spent
his time and dollars trying to improve. He had improved
them, too. Each acre that he had to release before he had
gone through The Gate was better in every respect than it
was when he had first obtained it. Each acre had received
his loving care.

There would be a stone up for him at Plum Grove in
the Powderjay plot, close to his mother, father and
brothers, and it would have his name, dates of birth and
death. Shan knew what his epitaph would be. He had
written it (with a little help from Robert Burns and John
Masefield) while he was in college but he didn't know he
was writing an epitaph.

> If there is life beyond the grave,
> He lives in future bliss.
> If there is not another world
> He made the most of this.

These were the words Jean had selected for his stone.
They would be cut in his granite headstone, inward and
deep so Time and the elements couldn't erase them for a
century or two. These words didn't seem right. Shan Powderjay was a college freshman and too young to be certain
when he wrote his epitaph. Like most all of his young
classmates, his head was filled with doubts.

Shan had not seen one of his classmates here. He had
created them in such minor details so far and long ago, he
doubted he would have known a single one unless it were
Flint Sycamore. Many were now passing through the Plum

Grove Gate he could not recognize. As Shan looked out upon and over them, going hither and thither among the stones, standing in groups, happy in their conversation and with much laughter he wondered if head creation was not better than flesh-and-blood. So many of his head children had lasted so long—and were so much alive. Other people's head children had lived over three thousand years. Shan had often wondered if one of his three or four thousand would reach the ripe age of two thousand years. It could happen to people created by the word.

His children were still coming up the hill. Now the Plum Grove City of the Dead was filled with his children, too close to stir about. They were almost touching each other. The Plum Grove Churchyard was filled. To have more freedom of movement, many were in Young's pasture field which was on three sides of Plum Grove's City of the Dead. They could look through the fence.

His children had about all arrived. There were a few singles, twos and threes coming up the hill now. There was Shan among them. He stood by, as if guarding the Plum Grove Gate. Gates were very important in one's life. There was one he went through, when he was born, from the unknown into the flesh-and-blood life upon his good earth either to be a constructionist and a success or a destructionist and a failure. There were only two classes of people upon the earth.

There was the second Gate he passed through from Life to Life, if he had kept the faith. If he had been a believer. If he had believed as Shan had believed. There was the word. And the word was not blue April wind. The word said something else. The word pointed a way. Then, there was something from the word—that everything had to come from within. It did have to come from within. Shan had always thought if people had had the faith, if they had believed, if they followed their Kingdom from Within, how wonderful the world would be. What a wonderful world it could have been with a foundation of the Kingdom Within, all the way back as long as there had been people.

His thinking changed as he saw the hearse rounding the curve at the foot of the Plum Grove Hill. He knew King was at the wheel and Big Thomas was beside him. It was hard to explain why a man would want to be a mortician. Why would somebody like Big Thomas want to lead a long train of sorrow to a chapel or church? After the services he saw to it sorrow went with the sealed husk underground where it would be buried forever. Each spring the resurrected grass would grow and green earth's scar.

In this hearse was Shan's husk with temporary and dignified sorrow from Jean, Janet, his brother, three sisters and other relatives, nieces, nephews, a few great-nieces and nephews, and several in-laws. There would be some strangers who had come from other places, unknown to his family and friends. They had come because Shan's children had been their friends, enclosed by the covers of a book, which lay on a table handy or by their favorite chairs to turn to on evenings. His books were often on stands near bedsides where they were kept to read and reread. People in words he had preserved and hoped to perpetuate, if he could, as Ralph Waldo Emerson, Robert Burns and many other old friends had done for Shan. He had kept their books by his chair, by his telephone (when he was making long calls) and on a small stand by his bed.

Had he returned to others the favor Burns, Emerson, Thoreau and Whittier had done for him in his younger years? If so, this was great achievement!

Behind the hearse was the white Cadillac in which Jean had rushed him, twenty miles in twelve minutes, to Kingston Hospital when he was in all that pain on the early morning of April fifth. Shan wondered what the time was now. For him there was no sun to tell time by. He didn't have his watch which would be on his left wrist. He couldn't tell time, had no need to tell where there was no time. Time was standing still. All time was the same. This way there was no rush by people. Rushing, tension and worry gave so many people heart attacks.

Shan knew Jean would be in this car. Janet would be in it. His son-in-law, John Meyers, could be driving—while his grandsons, Conrad and Markstrom, who loved their grandfather, whom they called by his first name Shan, were in the rear seat with their Grandmother Jean. These were the closest flesh-and-blood people to Shan on his earth. Janet was his only flesh-and-blood child. Conrad and Markstrom were his direct flesh-and-blood descendants.

Behind the white Cadillac were a number of cars flying little white flags as they came up the hill, their engines groaning in low. The hearse, as it came up the hill, was in bulldog low, and groaning under pressure of the climb. It pulled up on the flat hilltop where the engine breathed a sigh of relief. Then it pulled over near the Chapel.

Big Thomas was first to get out. Then King, who was driving the hearse emerged. King and Big Thomas had rushed Shan to the Intensive Care Unit at St. Ann's in Hummewell, West Virginia, three times, his second, third and fourth attacks. They had rushed him to the Intensive Care Unit, Kingston Hospital, Auckland, on his fifth attack. Only on his first and sixth attacks had Big Thomas and King not got to him first. Now they had brought his husk to Plum Grove Chapel for the last ride. Here would be remarks about him, then he would be laid to sleep forever with his family, friends, and enemies forever and forever. It would be a long time. Now, Shan knew going through The Gate had been going into something rich and strange.

Shan changed his place now as he walked over from where he had been standing by the Plum Grove Cemetery Gate across the churchyard where cars were pulling in and parking. Real flesh-and-blood people were getting out. They couldn't see Shan but he certainly could see them. His head-birthed children were all over the place. Shan could see and hear his children who had come because their father was dead. They had come to see him laid to rest in his native earth. His head children were certainly unaware he was among them. They had never known him in the flesh. They had had no occasion to memorize their father's image.

Shan's new standing position was at the east window of the Plum Grove Chapel. The back of the Chapel was north. The entrance faced the south. Shan was at the rear-north window on the left side where he could look in at the pulpit, podium, organ and where his body, his husk, would be last viewed. The coffin lid would be raised. And a line of viewers would, some few would not, walk up, look him over, lying there, then return to their seats.

The last to have the final look, who would linger longest, would be Jean, who had worked so faithfully during six attacks to keep him alive. She had been the closest to him of any person he had known on this earth.

Now as he found the right spot where he could look and see through the window he could hear and view everything with his own eyes.

He wondered as he stood there watching and waiting. What if all the people gathered inside the Chapel could see him standing out there looking in, 225 pounds of flesh, bone, blood and muscle, his hair crow-wing black and a little long when it should have been short as was the style in his day and time. One thing he had always been advanced on was haircuts. What if they could have seen him in his blue serge suit with double-breasted coat, his white shirt, black tie, tied in a knot such as only he could tie. Yes, see him in his black-laced shoes and his heavy black wool socks. What if all the people now coming inside the Chapel could see him through the window!

He smiled when he had this thought for he believed they would run down the double aisles and through the two front doors. He thought many of the more physically active doubters and unbelievers would raise the windows and jump from them. After they got out at the windows, they would hit the ground running faster than their legs could carry them. Those who would take to the aisles and doors would get back in their cars in a hurry and zoom off the Plum Grove Hill fast enough to turn over at the curves.

But, one thing about it, they would not see Shan Powderjay. They had no way. If they could see him standing there, he would have frightened all of them and many would be so scared they would have heart attacks.

Down the church aisle on the right side facing the church entrance, the aisle on the east side of the church, came the pallbearers. And what was pall? Shan thought. It was covering for a coffin. It could be a coat. It could be a blanket of smoke, fog, pollution that overcast the beautiful earth from a beautiful sky. There was none of this now. The earth was as beautiful as Shan had ever seen it. There was that beautiful blue—maybe with a touch of green like the rare harmless little green snakes that lived on bugs and insects. It was a beautiful color from earth as high as eternity was high.

Pall, Shan knew was everything it should be here. Pall could be to lose strength. Shan knew he was stronger right now than he had ever been in his life. It could mean to lose life. Shan knew he had won his second life by losing his first.

Shan knew definitely that pall was the wrong word, even if it did mean his husk and steel casket now coming up the aisle with seven bearers. There were three on each side and one walked at the head of the heavy casket, lifting with both hands. Seven bearers were toting a husk, enriched rented dust from the magnificent earth which wasn't pall, never had been and never would be. Shan's husk was now being returned to his true mother.

His bearers of his enriched resignation were people who didn't surprise him. His tall brother Finn, and four brothers-in-law, one married to Shan's youngest sister, Julia, Herendon Leonard, Linville Denton, ex-brother-in-law, had been married to Shan's second sister Mallie. They were divorced, but Shan had always liked Linville and their three children, Roberta, Beatinest and Nellie. Jean had seen to this, knowing his feelings. Not a bearer had been requested by Shan.

Then, there were two brothers-in-law on Jean's side, Gaston Cook married to Jean's third sister, Nanette, and there was Reed Cantrell married to her youngest and fourth sister, Laura. Her second sister, Chlotine, had lost her husband Ronald Zeblon ten years ago. He didn't survive the first attack.

Walking across from his Uncle Finn, was Shan's son-in-law, tall handsome John Meyers who, along with daughter Janet, had been citizens of the world. They had taught school in six countries. They had lived in five and traveled in seventy. The bearer at the head, Don Webber, was no blood-and-flesh kin to Shan but at Maxwell High School he had been Shan's coach and teacher, the greatest he had seen at that time of all who had ever worked with him. He was not a brother in the flesh, but he was a brother in spirit and a great constructionist. He had been from youth until now a much-needed man upon this earth. His Jean had chosen well. Shan, looking at his bearers, had no fault with them.

Under Big Thomas' and King's direction, the casket covered with a spray of lilies of the valley, was placed on a wagon that could be rolled directly in front of the pulpit. This was the regular routine in the Plum Grove Chapel as it had been since Shan could remember. Shan watched the Chapel fill up. His Jean, with sorrow on her face, her large blue-green eyes misty, with Janet and John Meyers, and grandsons, sat up on the front row. Family members piled in behind. Nieces, nephews on Jean's side and Shan's side —their children and some few of them their children's children. There were cousins, first, second and third, until all the center between the aisles was filled with flesh-and-blood family, close and little akin. More had come than Shan had expected would be there.

There were seats on either side of the Chapel between the aisles and three windows on each side. In these were people from Shan's valley, where he lived, and from his Little Methodist Church in Greenwood, which he had renamed jokingly as Refugee Church. He was once an outsider living in his community and town and he went to this church for protection. No one had ever followed him to Refugee Church to harm him. His purgatory had been living, disdained and feared until the people knew him better. Because what he had created from his head had been strange to them, there were many of his creations people didn't like. Many people who couldn't read or write had said they disliked them. They showed their power and influence by talking against Shan.

One mile away from where Shan stood he had first seen the light of day; four miles away in Greenwood he had taken his bride Jean Torris; here at Plum Grove lay his dead, and he would lie among them on the loving breast of one of his eternal hills.

Shan had felt warmly toward all of the fifty people who attended his church. He had perhaps felt kinder and warmer to them than they had toward him. He had attended irregularly because his lectures, his travels and teaching had taken him away over America and into so many foreign countries. He had never been as active as so many of the few men had been in his Little Church. He had never tithed. Had he, on certain years, he could have given enough to support the church. Why should he do it all? There were others who wanted to support the church, who did support it. Contributions from small to large from the few members they had supported his Little Church.

Yes, they had come from Greenwood here, perhaps as a duty and not out of love for him, to the little town where his Jean had grown to womanhood, had taught school; yet, after her marriage to Shan Powderjay, she dropped out of three national women's organizations where she felt unwanted after remarks by certain ones among them about her husband's books and stories. Up until his last and sixth heart attack, there wasn't a couple for them to travel with or to visit; however, they spoke to and were friendly with all.

Since Shan was less active than most people in his church, his faith had been doubted. He told one doubter who questioned him once he didn't wear his faith on the sleeve of his Sunday shirt. Shan explained to him but the man couldn't understand that the Kingdom of the Creator of the Universe was within him! When he said this to the man, he backed away! He didn't want any more of Shan and from this time on he remained shy of Shan and hostile to him. Shan saw him carried through the gate into the cemetery.

Shan looked through the window and he saw Odder and Alice Timmons on the front seat, between aisle and window on the far side of the chapel. Shan was glad they were there, for he remembered when he and Jean married they spent their honeymoon days at Alice and Odder's cottage on Front Street. Shan had also spent much time at their home working on books. As he looked at Odder, he thought of things that had happened to him in Heisel's Drugstore. Due to his Harvest, Plow, Hill and Story people, who walked the Greenwood streets, great animosities arose against him. He became a marked man and received threatening letters. He couldn't understand why he had received them. He wasn't trying to hurt anyone. He just had a dream of life—a positive dream. It was to portray people of his home and region as they were in his day and time. To portray and to create people, places and things. This was what he was doing. He was giving birth to many of his head children who were here today to see their father buried. Shan had learned that an idea could be a dangerous thing. He had learned when he was a young flesh-and-blood man of great physical strength and power that a dream could get him killed. Since he had such great strength and endurance, such good fists that could strike like lightning, he feared no man physically.

He learned, with his back turned to the room when he ordered a Coke at this very fountain, where he had been sitting with Everett and Odder Timmons. He was hit over the head three times with a heavy weight blackjack. His head was laid open to the skull in three places and bleeding. His crow-wing heavy black hair was red with his blood. The licks dazed him but in a half memory he knew his assailant. He reverted to the animal instinct in man. He turned and had him by the throat and had choked his tongue out. Three men unloosed his death grip around his assailant's throat by prying his fingers loose and pulling them up and back in a hurry.

Shan was rushed to General Hospital in Toniron, Ohio, by a friend. The gashes were cleaned and the skin fastened

back with cleats to cover the white skull. He was held over-
night there. A cousin, A. O. Shelton, walked over the Ohio
River bridge from Rosten, Kentucky, to see him. A beautiful young schoolteacher, Jean Torris, drove up from Greenwood to see him. She was the only human being outside his
first cousin A. O. Shelton and his brother, sisters, father,
and mother to see him. At that time, due to many of Shan
Powderjay's head children who were now gathered on the
Plum Grove Hill to see him buried today, flesh-and-blood
people didn't care for Shan Powderjay in their midst. Too
many wanted him gone. What if he had died then and
could not have created all these children who were around
him now? This had happened to him in Heisel's Drugstore, center of all activity of his sacred spot on earth, his
county, his Valley and Plum Grove Hills. Greenwood was
center and capital.

He had had his fourth heart attack in Heisel's Drugstore. That was on a day when he was asked to come and
autograph his books. He was placed at a table with people
all around him. A woman who didn't want to buy a book
crowded ahead of others and stood over him talking as fast
as a whirlwind telling him how rotten the people were in
Appalachia and how terrible he was. This lasted an hour
before a woman from Cincinnati shushed her with a hand
over her mouth. Shan had broken out in a sweat first. Then
he thought it might be angina but he didn't want to put
N.G.'s under his tongue in the presence of forty people
around the table. The pain became so severe Paul Artines,
a classmate and friend, too, took him at seventy in his car
to his home in the Valley. Here with more N.G.'s and
Scotch on ice with branch water which didn't help, Jean

called Big Thomas and King and they took him to Kingston Hospital. Blackjacked almost to death, a heart attack and a threatened suit all in this Heisel Drugstore, center of his community life and the place where he bought twenty-two pills he had to take per day. He had done this for twenty-two years. He wasn't taking those pills now. He didn't have to take them. He was full of health and strength again. The blackjack only left scars on his head. What the woman had said to him didn't matter. He was free from heart attacks, too.

When his brother, son-in-law, Don Webber and brothers-in-law carried his steel casket up and placed it on a roller table before the pulpit, Shan watched the young Reverend Edward Wilton walk up on the podium. Reverend Wilton had a young wife, an elementary teacher, who had taught to help her minister husband through the seminary. He had graduated from Oral Roberts University. Shan had always had more faith in this young minister of his small church than he thought his minister had in him.

Nine out of ten men were more active in Shan's church than he. But here Shan stood outside among his children now, who stood in silence with heads bowed while Reverend Wilton stood behind the pulpit inside and said a prayer. His prayer was for the soul of Shan Powderjay. He didn't say in his prayer where Shan Powderjay was or would be. This didn't matter to Shan Powderjay, who stood outside the church window, watching and listening to all proceedings.

He was tall enough to look inside at his minister, his wife, daughter and kin and all the flesh-and-blood people there from Greenwood, W-Hollow and a few surrounding

areas. There were a few strangers among the people he
knew. Counting the minister and his wife, the six in the
choir who came from his church in Greenwood, all of his
flesh-and-blood kin and his kin by marriage, there could
have been one hundred flesh-and-blood people crowded
into this small chapel.

While his minister prayed Shan looked in at the window at his steel coffin wherein was the husk of him, that
well-used husk which he had no desire to see. He was
listening to his minister, so very young with a boyish face.
It didn't matter what he said in his prayer, about him and
for his soul, before his flesh-and-blood kin, his in-laws,
friends and strangers who had come for their own individual reasons. Regardless of what the preacher said Shan
knew the man he was from within. He was that man who
had come from the Kingdom Within.

Long ago he had known it was vanity to take a name in
vain. A great name taken in vain showed the participant's
weakness of trying to show his greatness by dethroning the
Creator of the Universe.

Shan knew, too, how he had loved his parents. He
knew how they had loved him. He was one and the same
with his mother and father and all of his life he had given
to them instead of taking from them. He had bought medicine for them in their last days before they had gone
through The Gate. He had seen his mother and father
maybe three hours ago—for his time wasn't measured now.
He had talked to his father and mother. He would soon be
seeing them again. He didn't have to be told to honor them.
He had always honored his father and mother since he

could remember. They had brought him through The Gate to Life.

He had never killed a man. He was prepared to kill a man once who was going to kill him. He was the man who had hit him over the head in Heisel's Drugstore in Greenwood with a piece of steel. He went armed with two loaded revolvers on his person. He came face to face with his assailant on a Greenwood street. When he met the man his trigger finger was on a loaded gun. His assailant walked on past in deathly silence. Shan looked over his shoulder to see he didn't turn and fire. What if he had killed him? He often thought he could have never afterward lived with himself in peace. There was that Kingdom Within him that had to be lived in. He was happy he hadn't taken a human life.

He was happy because he had a reverence for life. He hadn't hunted since he was a grown man. The last wild-life he had killed was a squirrel for his mother and father. Mick was dying and requested broth from a squirrel. Shan had written unpopular poems about his country's fighting useless wars. Shan Powderjay didn't kill anything but copperheads and rattlesnakes. Because he had been a non-killer, he thought, because he had had such great reverence for life was one of the reasons why he was so much alive and standing here.

Women had appealed to him from the time he was small. Shan had been a very masculine man. He loved the feminine voices of women. He loved the company of women. He also knew women, if in control of their countries, would never start wars and get their men killed. So

many wonderful, beautiful, nice women he had met at
home and in foreign lands. For him, there was one woman
now. She was Jean. She was sitting in the church. He was
looking at her now. She had been the talented woman he
loved, one who had fought to extend his physical life. However, Shan Powderjay was like all other he-men; he had
lusted, but this was only for a little while. The passing of
time had taken care of lust of the flesh. He had never taken
unfair advantage of any woman.

Maybe he had driven a few hard bargains in life, but
not as many as had been driven against him. He had never
stolen anything. He had been as honest to the penny as he
knew how to be. He knew other people had to live, too.
Why should he take from them? Well, he hadn't, and he
had lived well in his later years. He had land, stocks, cash
deposits in banks. He had lived as well as he had wanted to
live but never had seen all countries in the world which
had been his aim. He had been so right now, he knew,
about the accumulation of wealth. He was empty-handed.
He didn't have his billfold in his hip pocket. Right now he
didn't need it. He had worn clothes on his body to hide
his nakedness. He had good wool socks on his feet which
had been cold so often in his later years! And he had shoes
on to protect his feet because he had done a lot of walking. He needed shoes on his feet.

Certainly one thing, he had never been jealous of what
his neighbors had. He had never coveted one thing a neighbor had! Why should he have coveted anything? He had
what he wanted. He had worked hard and long to get it.
But working hard and long he had accumulated much his
neighbors wanted. Still, why had people been so jealous of

him? They had been jealous, even those who lived along hard-surfaced roads, were jealous and wrote him nasty unsigned letters when a hard-surfaced road was built through *his* valley. This made it possible for him to drive a car in and out the year around. He was one of the last to get a hard-surfaced road in his county. This was something that had to come. Strangers from many states, who knew the children he had created, children with him today, had come to see his valley.

He had not written unsigned letters to anyone despite his getting hundreds of these over the fifty years he had created people, places and things on paper. When he sent a letter his name was on it. If and when he ever had a letter in a paper or magazine his name was on it. These letters were fighting for causes, a new County Health Department, a new County Park, new County Libraries. They were constructive letters. They were building letters. They were never to tear humanity down. They were written to help people live better lives. Shan couldn't believe he'd be getting any more of these destructive letters now. All of these little thunderings of humanity against him were over. What the minister had said in his prayers were good words.

His minister was one of the three male voices in a choir of six in his small church. After his prayer, Reverend Wilton joined the choir. They sang "Creator of the Universe, How Great Thou Art." Shan had always wished he had written these words and music. These were the right words and the right music.

Shan watched Jean, Janet, John and his grandsons. Jean he watched most. She had the stateliness and the dignity of a queen. Her eyes were misty for she had suffered much. Jean knew Shan's life as no other person. She knew the pains he had suffered. She was always with him, with his medicines—was always preparing choice foods on his diet. She was always dressing up his head children on paper, seeing that they were in character. She had given them names, too. She had worked beside him almost around the world. She had designed and decorated, furnished with nice antique pieces from states at home and countries around the world, a home people came to see. Jean had put it together. There had not been many things she could not do. Shan's tall and beautiful Jean always dressed in the best of taste.

She didn't see Shan standing there looking in at the window. She didn't see Shan's children, either, covering the churchyard and beyond as close as they could stand. They were crowded up against the church looking in at the six windows and two open doors. Shan's way now and had been, except when with his parents, to stand back and look over all. It was his situation all the way.

There was a stillness in the Plum Grove Chapel. There was seriousness on every face as the choir sang "Creator of the Universe." This was a great moment for Shan Powderjay. This was a time of exaltation! He stood as high as his universe was high. He was above and beyond those who had tried to degrade him. He was glad now that he had stayed here, lived here and had never let himself be forced to leave. How many men had ever been privileged to hear a prayer said for them, a song sung and a funeral preached? How many had ever attended their own funerals?

The Plum Grove Hills, W-Hollow could erode, and blight could kill the beautiful trees of many varieties on his farm. Wind could blow the earth away. The flesh-and-blood people of earlier years and his own generation who had spent their time fighting him, who had never created head children themselves, would be gone forever.

What he had done with head-born children, standing here today all over this hilltop, looking in at the windows, thousands of them who had come in from all over his state and country and from all over the world, would never be erased. It didn't matter now how some, maybe many of the flesh-and-blood people had fought him. He was there, secure, standing straight and tall and full of health. He wasn't bragging when he thought this. His thinking was good. His mighty Kingdom was Within.

When the song was finished, young Reverend Wilton read from his text. "I am the resurrection and the life." Then he commenced his funeral oration for one of his church who was deceased. This was in the same pattern as hundreds of others that had been preached at Plum Grove. There were over a thousand sleepers and dreamers lying here with and without stones. Some things he was saying could have been corrected by Shan who was listening to his words. When the brief sermon was over for a man born of this earth's durable soil, who had lived a rich and rewarding life despite the people who had tried to destroy him, Reverend Wilton said a second prayer. And, after his prayer, people in the Chapel could take a last look at Shan Powderjay's husk, unfamiliar to many. Shan had seen so much of this routine here at the Plum Grove Chapel he had known since the beginning of his life.

Big Thomas opened the casket lid. He propped the lid up high. Big Thomas' assistant King stood close beside

him. Shan watched many people file by his bier. Their
faces were serious and curious as they took a last look at the
man who had been in their midst. Shan watched the long
line slowly file past. Many of the people in this Chapel
didn't go past his steel casket to view his last remains.

After the non-kin, most of Shan's in-laws and kin filed
past to see his husk for the last time on earth. This was silly,
too, so thought Shan who was looking in. The real Shan
Powderjay was watching all of what had happened and
knew it was vanity. Then there were Shan's brother, his
sisters and in-laws. They passed slowly and without excitement. This was just another funeral. The sooner it was
over, the better it was for all concerned.

Last to review the husk was the immediate family, Jean,
Janet, John Meyers and his grandsons. They walked by in
single file. They didn't linger very long. They knew death
was as much a part of life as birth had been. They knew
after birth, death was inevitable. This was the way it was.
This was the plan of the universe. After a last prayer was
said by Reverend Wilton, it was over in the Chapel.

The pallbearers now came up and they carried Shan's
husk out of this Chapel, which he had attended as a boy.
They carried it across the churchyard with people following through the Plum Grove Cemetery Gate toward the pile
of fresh dirt. Big Thomas and King opened the cemetery
gate so the pallbearers could go through walking slowly
toward the big hole in the Plum Grove earth and the high
pile of dirt.

Shan's children moved from the churchyard and filled
Plum Grove's City of the Dead. Shan followed most of the
flesh-and-blood people who walked over into the cemetery.

They came to hear his last rites, "dust to dust" as his young minister crumbled a clod of the fresh upturned sod. They watched Shan's steel casket let down into the concrete vault. Shan stood over in the cemetery by the stone of one of his characters, Sonnie Villers, who was buried between his two wives. The Plum Grove dead could not come to life and sit on their mounds of earth to watch Shan Powderjay laid to rest. He was put down in that hole of Plum Grove earth.

Big Thomas said: "You may go now. We will fill in the grave. We will take care of the rest."

Shan had stood aloof in the Plum Grove Cemetery. He had watched the powerful man he had been, now silenced and laid to rest forever in the Plum Grove earth. Shan watched the departing crowd leave the Plum Grove City of the Dead in single file. He watched them file through the gate going to their parked automobiles. Now, it was all over.

Shan's children began to depart. He watched them leaving the top of the Plum Grove Hill by the twos, threes and by the dozens. They left this Plum Grove City of the Dead. They began walking off the hill, down the winding road on their way back to Three Mile.

Shan didn't leave the Plum Grove Hill with his children. He stood watching Big Thomas' men, who were Plum Grove men, shovel the dirt in on his steel casket in its concrete vault. He watched them fill the hole with loose dirt with their spades. He watched them heap the dirt into a mound over his husk, a mound like that over his father, his mother and brother. This Plum Grove City of the Dead was a lonely hilltop.

Shan watched his flesh-and-blood kin and others leave the hilltop. His Jean, his daughter Janet, her husband John and grandsons were slow and reluctant to leave. They left in sorrow but with dignity. Shan liked this. They were not weeping. Why should they weep? This was silly. How could their weeping help anything? It couldn't.

Shan stood there in the cemetery beside one of the graves while he watched thousands of them leave the Plum Grove Hill. He watched nearly one hundred flesh-and-blood people leave this hilltop. Shan stood alone looking at the mound of fresh upturned earth which was his. Shan had heard and he had seen himself planted forever in the Plum Grove earth. He was there with his mother, father and brother. There was a place beside him for Jean. There was a place for Janet and John and their sons. This was the way it should be after their joys and sorrows of traveling all over the earth. There was a time for everything. This was the time of finality. Without possessions they must come to this. Their husk finality was in this Plum Grove earth, a lonesome, forlorn, quiet hilltop.

Shan stood alone on this hilltop near the gate. He watched John and Janet go with his Jean, go with his grandsons to the white Cadillac. He watched them get in the car and drive slowly from the hill. What his father and mother had told him was to come to Three Mile to meet Huey the Engineer's train. They didn't tell him what it was that he would see. Now he had been glad that he had come. He was overjoyed that he had seen.

Shan had watched the four men employed by Big Thomas shovel the last loose dirt into his grave. Two men shoveled from each end of the loose pile. They had this job to do. They did it in a hurry. The last loose dirt they made into a mound and patted the top, side and ends with their spades so the clods would not roll down. Then they carried the canopy to their truck. Speaking in low tones to each other the four returned to place on the grave a blanket of flowers which had not been carried into the small Chapel. They were the last to leave this Plum Grove City of the Dead. Shan watched them get into their truck, three up front, one in the truck bed with the shovels and then drive off over the hill. Shan would be the last to leave. He had seen everything take place. He had thought all had gone according to custom. His Jean had planned everything well.

All through Shan's days from young manhood until now, he had always had positions of responsibility. He had never trusted his place of responsibility to others. He had always known if he could be there and attend to his responsibility, all would go well. He thought of the intense love and care he had given school properties where he was a principal—how he had cared for his classroom when and where he was a teacher. He knew how he had improved his forests by setting trees and keeping away forest fires.

This had always been a part of that positive feeling which had come from within.

He had remembered what uneducated Old Annis Bealer used to say about thinking through steel. Shan had called it concentration and meditation. He could be alone sitting under the shade of a tree, feeling the cool wind on his face and here he could unravel a thought from beginning to end. Here, he could put a story together in his head, create a dozen children in the story which he would put on paper later. It could be ten years later before he put his ideas on paper. They were in his head. He had created them. He would not forget them. Once he waited seventeen years to put on paper story children that were acceptable to a magazine with the greatest fiction reputation in the United States. For this story and the head-born people he had created he received the most money he had ever received for a story. Five thousand for a day's work had been good pay.

Everyone now had gone from the hill but Shan. He was the last to start walking out of the cemetery. He looked at the stones in rows—white stones as clean as a hound dog's teeth. These white stones were pretty in the green wine-wind of April. This wind was so good to breathe. This was Plum Grove wind, singing over the low hilltops, through the barren twigs of the oaks, and needles on the arms, hands and fingers of the pines. Winds, he knew, had always blown incessantly here. These winds were flavored like good foods Jean had cooked for him. Too bad, Shan knew, these winds couldn't touch any part of his husk planted down in Plum Grove earth, enclosed in steel and the steel enclosed in concrete. The winds he had loved blowing over here so much and so often would never touch his old self, never again, throughout all eternity. Old winds could blow over from the level of the hilltops in all directions as they had blown forever. They would continue, these beautiful wine-green eternal winds. Winds that had flavor to breathe and to blow into infinity.

This eternal spot belonged to Shan. He knew this as he was departing. Even if not all of it belonged to him, a little part did. What did he want with all of it since he had his

Kingdom Within? He had come into this world without anything. He hadn't brought land with him except the eight pounds of living, borrowed, baby-crying dust that he was. He had returned this with added pounds he had accumulated. He had given everything back. All possessions he had ever earned and accumulated had gone or would go to someone. Some of it would be destroyed by time and the elements. All of himself would go but his new self, his Kingdom. He was still on this Plum Grove Hill. He was still in command. Shan knew he was still as high as wind was high—as tall as all eternity. He was as positive as the hills around him. He was as positive as the millions of stars he had seen in an ice-blue, moonless sky, about two o'clock on a frosty morning in October.

Walking now, he wasn't trying to play catch-up with all the others. The long line of automobiles had moved off. The majority of drivers had only a short distance to go. This had been just another day for many. It had been just another funeral for one in their midst, held in the little church where one was supposed to attend.

There had been a book for people to sign in Big Thomas' parlor in Greenwood where Shan had reposed for an evening. This was the way it was done. Shan wasn't conscious of having been in Big Thomas' parlor. He had had such a hard time escaping Kingston Hospital up in Auckland. He walked down the Plum Grove Hill, down that winding road with black and red haw bushes on the left side, growing from that infertile and eroded small area of earth. Shan knew one thing and he was positive about this, he wouldn't be caught in Kingston Hospital again. He wanted no part of needles, medicines, doctors. He had liked his nurses. He was especially fond of little "Scrappie." He couldn't forget her slapping life back into some half-dead patients. Shan had had many nurses but he had to go along with "Scrappie!" She was a bright star above his green April wind.

Soon these short haw trees with their black iron tracery would put forth bud, blossom and leaf. They would bear fruit good to taste. Shan remembered how along this road he used to run as fast as he could after his day was over, in the one-room school that used to be up there on the hill over where he was planted now. He tried to beat Charlie Dials, Jimmy Felch and Morris Skinner to the trees to get haws that had ripened that day and had fallen to the ground.

He ran past the Annis Bealer bottom that grew the tall corn, the hundred bushel per acre. Shan didn't care to remember that as much as he did the blue and white morning-glory blossoms on the vines that climbed the tall stalks. He had walked this way maybe four hours ago. No sun and no watch and he couldn't reckon time. He walked over the plank-covered bridge that spanned the stream by Annis Bealer's tall house with the steep roof.

Shan was walking over a road that had changed the least in his sixty-six years of knowing Greenwood County. This was an important road going to the Plum Grove Cemetery and Chapel and to many houses; yet, this road in places was too narrow for two cars to pass. It was still an old-fashioned Greenwood County dirt road that froze and thawed in winter until automobiles couldn't get over it.

Shan could walk over it, the only road leading to Plum Grove. This was the way his children had come and gone. Lucky for Big Thomas and King, for his flesh-and-blood kin, members of his church and others this road was dry today. There were no puddles of water. There were no ruts in this winding dirt road.

There was no one ahead of Shan. He had waited to watch the four men Big Thomas had brought do the last service for him at Plum Grove. He had let all the people go ahead of him. All were riding in automobiles. He had let his children go ahead of him. They filled the roads. There were hundreds and hundreds of them—maybe two, three maybe four thousand. They were a varied assortment of humanity. They were walking back to Three Mile to Huey's train. Some were walking back to Greenwood.

Now Shan walked upon the single-track railway. He looked down toward the station. There were only two people standing there. The train had gone. There were none of his head children waiting. They had gone. Shan stepped upon a T-rail where he could balance himself easily. Soon he recognized the pair at the station. His mother and father were back waiting for him.

"Shan, we told you," his father said. "You met Huey's train all right?"

"Oh yes, I met the train and I watched my children unload from the four coaches."

"You complained about your having only Janet," his mother said with a smile. "Now what do you think?"

"They were at Plum Grove with me," Shan said. "There were thousands there at my funeral."

"We've been here watching them leave," Mick Powderjay said. "I've flagged Old Huey many a time here at this station. I've not bothered him today. He's been a busy man shuttling back and forth to Riverton. He has seven coaches now! Your children rode on top of the coaches. They were hanging on the sides of the cars. They were between the cars riding on the couplings. They were up in the cab with Huey. They even rode on the cowcatcher."

"Malcolm Partlow has his train here helping," his mother explained. "He has been going forward down track with his Number Two train. Then, he has backed out to here. Huey pulls forward out with his Number One train here to Three Mile. Then Huey backs his train to Riverton. Both trains have seven coaches. Many of your children walked down the track toward Riverton and Greenwood. We saw all the last ones load on to the trains and go! And it's been something to see."

"Your children, Shan, remind me of the long trains of crows we used to watch fly over. There would be a flight of crows ten miles long and enough to darken the sun. They went over our house and farm on their way to roost in the pines across the Ohio River over at Hillhavens. Remember?"

"Sure do, I was a boy then!"

"We didn't go to Plum Grove," Shan's father told him. "We knew you would see to everything. We knew you would be over it all. You would have the place well in hand."

"That is true," Shan told his parents. "I have been in full command from the beginning until the four cleanup men patted down with their shovels the clods rolling from my mounded grave."

"Mick and I were standing here and watched Big Thomas and the long line of cars following him with their little white flags flying as they took you to Plum Grove, Shan," his mother said. "We knew he was taking your temple of clay—that the real you had been with us."

"Little Thomas, Big Thomas' father took your mother to Plum Grove with the white flags flying you will remember," Shan's father said. "That was the longest funeral procession ever to go to Plum Grove."

Shan had remembered his mother's long funeral procession when there were nearly as many flesh-and-blood people there as he had flesh-and-blood people and the children he had created, combined. He didn't attend his father's funeral for his father's heart gave out and he walked through The Gate while Shan was hospitalized in his home after days and weeks in a real hospital. Shan had never seen his father buried. He had just missed him after he convalesced and learned to walk again. He had gone through The Gate on his way into Time.

"Plum Grove," his mother exclaimed.

"Plum Grove," his father repeated.

Plum Grove was a special place on the earth. It was a small part of the earth which the Powderjays knew best. It was that bed where they could sleep forever under the music of immortal winds blowing from infinity to infinity. Never would one of these eternal winds kiss a Plum Grove sleeper's face. Their beds were too deep and their quilts above them were too thick.

"It's wonderful to see you again," Shan told his parents. "You seem to be enjoying yourselves for once! You're happy, and having a good time!"

"No problems," his mother said.

"We knew you would return this way, Shan," his father said. "After the last loaded trains left we waited for you."

"We have a message," his mother said.

Shan stood there looking at his parents. His tall mother who had given him birth. Her olive-skinned face, her thick lips and big mouth and her crow-wing black hair. It was through her body he had come into this world. She had been and was everything in this world to him.

His father with the high forehead, the long roman nose, the large blue eyes, thin lipped, red faced, a small man whose voice carried. His father could laugh like a loud blowing wind over his Plum Grove Hills. How could he ever do anything but honor his father and mother, who had brought him into a world where he had had so much to learn and so little time. It had been a great adventure from beginning to end. From his flesh-and-blood had come that second self, his Kingdom from Within, powerful and ever-lasting.

"Mom, what is the message you have for me?"

"Shan, you have to go back and come again."

"Oh Mom, why do I have to do this?" Shan said with sadness in his voice. "I have never been so happy, enjoying my strength and living without pain. Crossing through The Gate from Life to Life has been great. Why do I have to go back and come again?"

Shan's mother didn't answer him.

"Sorry, Shan, but that is the way it is," his father said with a smile on his thin lips and his large blue eyes looked like they were filled with laughter. "Yes, that is the way it is—what your mother has told you."

Reverend Wilton, who was allowed to visit Intensive Care patients at any time, came unexpectedly.

Shan felt that he had seen him only a short time before, conducting his funeral at Plum Grove. Or had he? Had he really been there? Was he dreaming?

"How are you today, Shan?" Reverend Wilton asked.

"Just great," Shan said. "I have spent the afternoon with my parents."

"Oh, really?" Reverend Wilton was surprised. "I thought both parents were deceased."

"In reality, yes, they are," Shan said. "But in the dream world where I have been I was with them. It was a great meeting and I hated to leave them."

Shan stared thoughtfully into space. Reverend Wilton said goodby and left him.

Then Shan heard the good news that on this April twenty-seventh he would get to go home. He would have to go home in pajamas, wool socks and house slippers. He would have to live in his own home, dressed in pajamas, house slippers and wool socks and robe the few days left in April and all of May. Beginning the month of June he could go for short drives.

This morning was different from other mornings now in his private room. He had spent eleven days in Intensive Care and he had spent eleven days in his private room. In Intensive Care he had crawled over the top of his hospital bed and had had a good fall down to the floor and all the way to Plum Grove Cemetery. Then when he was moved to a private room Jean rented a hospital cot and spent nights in his room with him. He would listen to her voice and mind her even when half asleep or semi-conscious.

Once while in his private room he wouldn't eat hospital food. He ordered a steak. Doctor McAilster told Jean to get him a small steak. Shan relished every bite.

He hadn't remembered how his first eleven days had been spent in Intensive Care. He hadn't remembered any part of it though in sickness and in health he had always had a retentive memory. He could remember faces, places and things but never mathematical formulas. He hadn't remembered his eleven days in Intensive Care this time as he had the last time, back in December of 1973 when he was here in Intensive Care.

This morning he was up early, had had his bath. He had shaved himself. Jean had brought the hot water for him to make lather to brush on his face. It was great to shave himself and not have one of the nurses do it. Darlene Kenton, the one who had given him physical therapy for the last eight days, had come and she had taken him for his walk. He walked with her down to the front desk where they turned right, angled down the corridor to an elevator. They went down on the elevator to a lower corridor. Here they walked on this corridor to an elevator. They came up to the second floor on this elevator and got off on a corridor that came in on the left side of the front desk. On this route they made a small circle. They went from the second floor down to the first. Not anywhere along this circuitous route was there a window where Shan could look out and see flowers blooming and leaves on the trees. He knew they had to be out there. Yet, the last flowers he had seen in bloom were the daffodils in his yard and along the lane road that were shown by his car lights on that early morning of April fifth. Here it was twenty-two days later in an April that would soon be gone and he'd not seen a bud, leaf or another blossom.

There was one thing he did remember about Intensive Care. He remembered that he was placed so far over—maybe about the middle of that vast room with patients all around, that there were no windows for any of them to look out to see the beautiful changing world outside. Shan had seen no flowers in Intensive Care. His publishers had sent him beautiful flowers which Jean had displayed in the Intensive Care waiting room. He saw these when he was wheeled out from Intensive Care to a private room. These few feet of travel in a wheel chair had been as great to Shan as flying from Kennedy Airport in New York across the Atlantic to Orly Airport in Paris.

Shan had hoped for a window in his private room. He got one with a window all right. He could look out on stone walls. There was a chimney stack that was constantly belching clouds of smoke toward the sky. Shan didn't like the window of his private room. Private rooms were hard to come by in this hospital. One had to wait to get one for somebody to die or be moved out in a wheel chair to go home. Shan had thought about quarreling about his window, then he decided against it. He had been lucky to obtain this private room. Twenty-two days of April Shan

Powderjay had missed. But it wouldn't be long now, if what Shan had heard were true that he would be going home today—probably in the afternoon.

Jean looked through his doorway to the front desk. She saw Dr. Benjamin McAilster. The front desk, Shan had learned, was an important stop for a doctor. When one stopped there and gave papers and received papers something happened to a patient in a private room. One had either died or one was going home. The same woman, a mother at seventeen across the corridor from Shan who had had clots in her lungs and screamed out in pain, was no longer there. She had either gone home or she had gone to a mortician's parlor.

"Shan, I think you'll soon be checked out," Jean said.

Then Jean smiled as broadly as his mother had smiled when he had been with her and his father.

Jean watched Dr. Ben McAilster walk up the corridor to Shan's room where he came in with a bundle of papers as thick as a college dictionary.

"Well, how are you this morning?" Dr. Ben McAilster asked Shan.

Here was a doctor of all the many Shan had had in the latter years of his life with the best bedside approach to a patient Shan had ever known. He couldn't look at a patient unless he smiled a natural smile. He was middle-aged, very handsome and always well groomed. His smile, his good manners, and kind words Shan thought were as good for his patients as the medicines.

"Shan, how about going home today?"

"Great," Shan exclaimed. "Great! Great! I can't believe it!"

"Well, I can hardly believe it either," he said softly holding onto his smile. "Your wife got you here in the nick of time. We thought we'd lost you and we did lose you but the shock treatment started your heart beating again."

"Did I get heart injuries on this last attack?" Shan asked him.

"You certainly did," he replied.

"I hate to hear that!"

"You've had six major heart attacks," Doctor McAilster told him.

There were two chairs in Shan's private room. Shan and his cardiologist sat facing each other. Doctor McAilster lifted the bundle of papers that looked to Shan like they could be the loose-typed manuscript pages of a very large novel.

"In all of your major heart attacks but one you've added more heart injuries," he told Shan. "In your fifth heart attack, though, it was a major one, you had less heart damage. You had more damage with your first massive attack which left your heart badly crippled. I'd say this last attack was second in damages to that first one."

"But I'm going to live, Doctor McAilster," Shan said. "I know I'm going to live! Heart damage or no heart damage, I'm going to live!"

"I like the way you think, but never let your positive thinking cause you to overdo."

"That something from within tells me," Shan said. "It is a positive voice. It is I! It is my second self! It is my Inner Self!"

Doctor McAilster looked at Jean, who was sitting on the end of her cot. His face was a bit serious when Shan mentioned that something from within was telling him that he was going to live. Shan had told Jean back when he was in Intensive Care when he had regained consciousness that he had received the word and that he knew regardless what his doctor or any other doctor said he was going to live. Shan also knew where he had been. He knew what he had seen. What he had seen and where he had been were positive facts. They were as positive as mountains were positive. They were as positive as wind bloweth where it listeth. He had seen his parents and had talked to them. He had been on a long and interesting journey. Where he had been and what he had seen wouldn't be good conversation to tell his busy cardiologist right now. Shan had never told Jean. Maybe he would tell her the whole story when they got home. Maybe not. Who were the people who would believe him?"

"We want you to keep your weight down," Doctor McAilster said. How many times had he said these words to broad-shouldered, big-framed Shan Powderjay. "We don't want you to have that seventh attack!"

"Maybe a seventh heart attack wouldn't be too bad," Shan replied with a smile. "A seventh attack could have its advantages."

Dr. Benjamin McAilster looked strangely at Shan. The smile left his face.

"It could be fatal," he said.

Shan made no reply to his comment.

Then that broad natural smile came over Doctor Mc-Ailster's face. That smile was like a sunrise up over the Plum Grove Hills. He held all the records and charts with both hands. He lifted them up and shook them to feel their weight.

"I would like to ask you something, Doctor McAilster," Shan said. "I want to know if you gave me sedatives to knock me out when I was rushed to the emergency room."

"Quite the contrary," he replied. "We never gave you anything to knock you out. All the time you were here in the hospital, we did all we could to stimulate your heart and sustain your life! My records show how you left this world and we revived you."

"Do you believe there is life beyond this life?" Shan asked him.

Doctor McAilster hesitated then said, "I have had patients who have told me of their personal experience after being brought back to life."

"Tell me, Shan Powderjay," he said with a joyous smile, "what you are made of! Six major heart attacks recorded here, and these have all been major ones! Yet you are here! So many men and women don't have the second chance! You tell me what you're made of!"

"I don't know, Doc," Shan spoke, greeting him with a forced smile. "You tell me. You're my cardiologist!"

"Yes, I am but talking to the patient after seeing all these records. It is an amazing thing for a cardiologist to contemplate!"

Shan didn't tell him. Shan wouldn't tell him. He had kept the faith. Shan had had to believe. Had he been born in Egypt five thousand years ago he would have believed in Horus or Ra Atem the beautiful sun god. Had he been born in Greece thirty-five hundred years ago he would have chosen the great Greek god Apollo. Shan had to believe. The Kingdom of God had always been within him. He had known when others thought, including his doctors, that he was going to die, an inner voice spoke the word to him that he was going to live. And he had lived. Would that inner voice speak to him again when his numbered years, months and days expired and he would pass through The Gate from Life to Life? He could not and would not speak his thoughts to his cardiologist. Had he spoken these thoughts, Doctor McAilster might have recommended a psychiatrist for him.

"Follow your diet, take your medicines as I have prescribed them for you. Stay in your home all of May in robe and pajamas! Later I will discuss short trips out in the car in June with your wife. Don't smoke any more cigars."

"No more cigars, Doctor McAilster," Shan said. "I have no desire. And I promise you, I mean this. No more of my wonderful cigars."

"No drinking."

"Yes, Doctor."

"No overeating."

"Yes, Doctor."

"Keep that weight down."

"Yes, Doctor."

"Don't climb steps."

"Yes, Doctor."

"Do all the walking you can do in your home and out in the yard, when weather permits. Walk on the level. Live in normal temperatures!"

"Yes, Doctor."

"Remember, we don't want that seventh attack. It could be the fatal one, you know."

"Yes, seven was always my lucky number. Don't worry about it. I won't."

"Well, this is it! Good luck to you, Shan! Keep in contact!"

Doctor McAilster got up from his chair. He smiled as he left Shan's private room, and hurried away. He was a busy doctor with very little leisure time whose life belonged to other people.

After Doctor McAilster left, Jean wrote a check for Shan's expenses which his insurance didn't cover. Counting what his insurance paid and he paid, he knew it didn't pay to be sick. It didn't pay financially to have the sixth heart attack. He had paid for it in two ways, cash and more heart injuries.

While Shan sat in his chair rejoicing, Jean was packing their belongings they had in this room. The biggest packing she had to do was getting the flowers together. He had a large basket filled with cards and letters. What he would take from this room would be very little—pairs of pajamas, an extra robe, two pairs of house slippers. While Jean packed he walked over to the only window in his room. He looked at the cold stone walls, at the massive chimney producing clouds of smoke that lifted into the air and thinned. This must have been the chimney for Kingston Hospital's heating plant.

When Jean had packed she went to the front desk and reported she was ready to go—and that she needed an orderly to wheel Shan through the corridors to the elevator,

down on the elevator and to the hospital door through
which they would leave. Shan had been over this route
before. He had been eager to leave last time, which was late
December. Snow covered the earth then. Now it was late
April and Shan, who was always out and alive with April,
couldn't wait to see birds on the branches of trees. He
couldn't wait to see leaves on the trees. He couldn't wait to
be out in April, the month of resurrection. He sat in his
room wondering what it would be like. He didn't have long
to wait. The orderly came with his wheel chair on which
there were places to load a few other items.

Shan was happy to get into this chair. He wouldn't
be helped. He was in his private room. He could do almost
as he pleased here. Jean laid a few things on the chair
and she carried the rest on the way out. Shan saw Darlene
Kenton, who was walking with another patient. He said
goodby to her, a young woman with whom he had had
many walks all in the corridors of Kingston Hospital where
there was not a window to look out and see the blossoms
and the leaves. Then, Shan waved to a nurse called "Red"
at the front desk.

In the corridor his orderly had to go slowly with his
wheel chair. There was a bed on rollers ahead with a
blanket over the sleeper. Here was one who hadn't made it.
This one was ahead of Shan's wheel chair. This one would
have an ambulance waiting for it. Shan would be going
down to a waiting car—the white Cadillac—that had
brought him here in a hurry. He would be leaving, slow-
paced and not in a hurry. The orderly moved Shan's chair
down on the same elevator with the covered body on
the rolling bed. Sure enough an ambulance was waiting.

Shan watched the ambulance driver and his helper load the blanket-covered figure into the ambulance and drive away. That one could have been him, Shan thought. But here he was alive and well and going home.

The orderly waited behind Shan in his wheel chair while Jean went to bring the parked Cadillac up where the living got in cars and ambulances took the dead to morticians.

Shan looked out in front of him. He couldn't believe what he was seeing. Trees in Auckland along the city streets were filled with leaves. He couldn't believe that April air outside the hospital in Auckland was so fresh and fine. He couldn't believe the freshness of the great April world that he was in. How wonderful the air was to breathe! It was fresh and fine and it tasted like wine in his lungs after he got out of Kingston Hospital.

Shan was so filled with excitement he tried to leave his wheel chair but his orderly, big, husky, much larger than Shan, put his hand on his shoulder and pushed him back in his seat. He didn't tell him in words but told him with his action: "You are not getting out of here until your car comes."

Then Jean drove up in a car both Jean and Shan said was their last car, perhaps, and their last fling with automobiles on the road. Shan wanted out of the wheel chair to the car. Again the big orderly pressed down on Shan's shoulder and he stayed in the chair. Then Jean got out and she and the orderly put Shan's and Jean's hospital possessions in the Cadillac. When Shan started to get out of the chair on his own, the orderly stayed him.

The orderly helped Shan from the chair into his car.

Shan thanked this man in his middle thirties for his kindness. Shan was now sitting beside his Jean, who was turning on a station of beautiful music on the radio. He hadn't heard this FM station since he had been hospitalized twenty-two days ago. Twenty-two days twenty years ago was a very short time. Twenty-two days now in Shan's present fast-moving world was a very long time. Shan wanted to hear beautiful music. He was hungry for it. He wanted to see birds, leaves and blossoms in this April. He was very hungry for these.

Jean drove from the Kingston Hospital loading zone where the fortunate living drove away and where the dead were covered over with sheets and ambulanced to morticians' parlors, of which there were a vast number in Auckland and vicinity.

As Jean drove out onto Lexington Avenue, Shan didn't know whether he was asleep and dreaming or whether he was awake, thinking, seeing, believing and not believing. Elms along the streets were fully leafed. Each tree top was a green cloud in the wind. And on this morning there was wind enough to rustle the green clouds of leaves to make them look like waves in the Mediterranean Sea blown up by the incessant blowing of the winds over Greece.

One thing that made Shan know he was very wide awake and his mind was active was that he wanted to get the true location of Kingston Hospital. He thought he had always known where it was since Janet their daughter was born here and Shan's mother had died here. After the experience he had had escaping from this hospital, he had a fixation in his mind it was high on a hill. But it wasn't on a hill. It was the same hospital where daughter Janet had been born thirty-five years ago and his mother Mollie Pow-derjay had died twenty-six years ago. As Jean drove down Lexington, Shan looked over to his left to see if there were a door, if there was an elevator on the hill. He knew he had come out at a door and walked down Lexington to Thir-teenth or Bridge Street as it was often called.

Jean wasn't driving fast. She was letting Shan, who had been released from hospital imprisonment where he had not seen the sun or felt an April wind blow on his face, had not seen a star, a bud, blossom or leaf for almost a month, savor his world. His favorite month had about passed since he went into Kingston Hospital and had been released. April was the month of resurrection and Shan Powderjay felt that he was being resurrected. His mind, always recep-tive to ideas when he was excited, was now filled and run-ning over! His crippled heart didn't feel that it was crippled now. It was overflowing with joy.

At the intersection of Lexington and Thirteenth or Bridge Street, Jean made a right turn. Shan was as positive that he had walked this way as he was that he was in the car that rushed him to the hospital and that he was coming home. Houses faced the street here, with yellow forsythia in bloom in some of the yards. Clusters of spirea in yards along this street had white blossoms. Some few had both yellow for-sythia and spirea blossoms. One yard had crocuses in bloom. When Shan had walked this way in early April these flow-ers were not blooming. Shade trees were fully leafed and all the yards had been mown. Shan knew he had walked this way.

"Jean, when you come to Carter, turn left and go down to Twelfth," Shan said.

"Not anything there but the old deserted Auckland Railway Station," she said.

"I know, but I want to see it again," Shan told her.

At Carter she turned left and drove from Thirteenth to Twelfth Street. Here was that deserted railway station with roofs over the platforms where passengers stood waiting for their trains. Here was the finest railway station ever built for a city Auckland's size. This beautiful stone depot was now being used for business offices. Shan knew that he had been here. His memory was correct. As sure as he was alive and breathing he had been to this railway station earlier this month.

"Thank you, Jean, for taking me by the station where I've caught trains for local and faraway places, New York so many times, Boston, Atlanta, Houston, Denver, St. Louis, Chicago, Los Angeles and San Francisco. Yes, many times for Philadelphia and Washington, D.C."

"It's a place of memories now," Jean told him.

She turned back onto Carter and drove down to Sixth. Here she drove over and connected with U.S. 23.

"As you know I've been driving back and forth home and if you think the trees and flowers in Auckland are nice to see, you wait until we get to the Valley. Wait until we get home."

"Just to see the sky, to see any kind of blossoms and green leaves trembling in the branches of trees—just to be out of that hospital and going home again! I think I must have had it this time. I think it was rougher than I have thought."

"It was rougher than you thought, Shan," she told him.

"You're very lucky to be going home with me. We're lucky to be together."

Shan could look from his window now over the tops of one industry after another at the broad and beautiful Ohio River. Despite industries occupying almost all available land between U.S. 23 and the Ohio River, he could see wild plums in bloom and leaves on the silver maple trees turned up by the wind. It was so much like riding a train out of Rome along the Tiber River, seeing the April resurrection he was seeing here. He had ridden that Italian train out of Rome in April. He was going to Florence. He had seen the silver of the upturned cottonwood leaves on the banks of the Tiber and along the tracks.

Very soon Jean was driving past the nondescript Rosten Railway Station. Shan had stopped here. Now, the four-lane superhighway by-passed Rutland. The railway tracks were midway between the Interstate and the river. The highway bordered the foothills. On Shan's right were houses and meadows. On his left were houses on acreages, some small hill and valley farms. Everywhere the slopes and valleys had trees. Their leafy tops were green sheets in the April wind. Here and there like round dots of white and red against the green, dogwoods and redbuds were in bloom. What a beautiful world this was. Kingston Hospital and all that had transpired there, Shan put behind him.

At State Route 1, Jean stopped for the signal light this time. A red signal stopped her. But she was not in any hurry. This journey home was a joy. It was not twenty miles in twelve minutes. State Route 1 passed the old Riverton Depot, post office and the beginning of Academy

Branch. State Route 1 with its world of green on either side
was coming nearer to Shan's world.

Two miles out to the Valley Road. Here Jean's face
brightened and she smiled as she turned right on Valley
Road into the Valley. It was here on this spot where the
Valley and State 1 roads intersected, was the old Three
Mile Station. It was here Shan had met Huey the Engineer's train. It was here thousands of his children material-
ized on the train and walked the rest of the way to their
father's funeral.

"Stop here for a minute, Jean," Shan said. "I want to
just look and think for a minute."

"Our Valley is an April paradise," she said. "We will
have two miles of this. You will see!"

Jean drove slowly up the hill. On the right side of the
road was Shan's farm. He looked up at the oak grove he had
kept underbrushed. Under the trees was still a carpet of
brown winter oak leaves while the tops of these oaks with
interwoven green branches formed a cloud roof of trembling
green and higher up and beyond this green leaf cloud was
an endless depth of cerulian blue sky.

"Ah, look, it's an April paradise," Shan said. "My
meadows! Look at the legions of grass all bending one way
—the way the wind blows! Think of winds influencing the
grass. Stop here!"

Jean stopped near the bend in the road. Here Shan
could look over the green meadow with white-barked syca-
mores on the far end and with the big twin hickory trees in
the center of the field. Then there was the largest meadow
in the Valley to his left.

"I want to sit here and absorb this green," Shan said.

"I've been resurrected from a prison into paradise. You're right! This is an April paradise."

On the hill slope above the big meadow on his left were white sails of blooming dogwoods moved by the wind. They were interspersed with red sails from the redbuds waving in the wind. And the woodlands all around the hickory nut tree bottom meadow, shaped like a horseshoe, were red and white sails against a canvas of soft, April-velvety green. This was Shan's April paradise. This was Shan's world and it was his farm. He was returning to it. He would not be away forever! He was returning. In front of the car and on the right Valley Stream wound slowly, quietly, peacefully around half of Hickory Tree Bottom Meadow.

"Ah, look, won't you, Jean," Shan exclaimed. "Do you see what I see coming up the bank?"

"A terrapin," Jean said. "He made it through a rough winter. The ground, so I read, froze twenty-two inches underground. You know a terrapin never goes that deep when he hibernates in earth for a winter's sleep."

The terrapin held his head high. His long neck and bony head were colored gold and black.

"It wouldn't surprise me if he's not just come out of hibernation," Shan said. "Down over the bank in that sandy earth would have been a good place for him to hibernate."

"Shan, you can't get out of the car and hunt for his place of hibernation," Jean said. "Remember Doctor Mc-Ailster's orders!"

"We'll watch him cross this road," Shan said. "There's not much traffic here but I'd like to see him safely across the road! He's going to the meadow over there where there is more clover."

In this meadow there was plenty of red and ladina clover, growing in fescue, the wonder grass. Shan thought this terrapin knew where he could find a vegetarian's dinner in April. Shan and Jean watched him across the road, stick the toes of his front feet into the bank and climb up to the meadow. When he climbed to the meadow, he began eating clover from among the legions of fescue, now blowing one way with the wind.

Now, Jean started the motor.

"We must move slowly on toward home," she said. "Aren't you anxious to be there?"

"I've never wanted to go home any more in my life than now," Shan told her. "To be here and to see all of this, I cannot absorb enough. I cannot see enough. And I can't contain all the thoughts I have about this. There will have to be more days and nights—more time."

The Valley meadows were divided by the Valley Stream into eleven creek bottom meadows. The Valley Road ran alongside the edge of the hill. Each creek bottom meadow Shan looked upon was greener than the ones he had just passed. On either side of the Valley the wooded slopes spread upward toward the blue.

"Ah, look out, there," Shan said. "Don't hit him!"

Had Jean driven on she would have run over him. She would have crushed him as the pretty blacksnake was crushed on the Womack Hollow Road. The big blacksnake, as long as Shan was tall, held his head high, looking in all directions with his forked tongue out of his hard-lipped mouth catching the sounds.

"There is resurrection in that pretty snake as old as the known world," Shan said. "I'd like to get out and catch him—let him crawl around my neck and over my shoulders. I've seen resurrected spring—first the terrapin and now the blacksnake."

"You're not getting out of the car, Shan," she told him. "We are going home!"

Shan watched the big snake crawl across the road to a pile of brush and logs. He crawled back under the logs.

"I couldn't get him now," Shan said. "He's out of sight!"

Around this sharp bend in the road there were white sails and red sails on three wooded hill slopes.

"The Valley has never been prettier!"

"And we're going home," Jean said. "We went away from here together. We're coming home together."

Jean stopped the car where Shan could look up his Valley and at the brown-and-oak–shingled house across Shingle-mill Hollow, a tributary to the Valley. Here was the long brown house with four white chimneys and black stacks to prevent down drafts of wind. Here was home. The two rows of golden daffodils from the Valley Road up to their home and alongside the walk up the hill from the house were gone. But here under the walnut grove Shan had set with his own hands were hundreds of white percoon flowers bending in the wind. Shan lowered the window in his door. He stuck his head out to breathe the natural fresh air of April. In all directions he looked the air was filled with bird wings. He had never seen so many wild birds of so many different species.

"What a great day for me," Shan said. "There was never a day like this. We have gone the circle. We left this place. Now we have returned."

Shan sat in the car on the drive where Jean had stopped.

He looked at the house. He looked at the green meadow above and below in the Valley. He looked at their green yard grass. He looked at multi-colored birds' wings fanning, slicing and cutting through the air.

Shan knew here was the beautiful earth where he had borrowed his accumulated living dust. He knew here was the place of beginning and eternal ending. He knew here was the beginning of that something from within. It had been there. It was there. And it would be with him forever.

"Look," Jean said. "Look who is coming."

Old Sugar Lump, their woodchuck, was up walking toward them on her short hind feet. Her forepaws were extended.

"She's resurrected from winter sleep from her home under our bedroom," Jean said. "She's wanting melon. We don't have it this early. We don't even have apples. But I do have pecans. She loves them. She's here to meet us."

Shan couldn't believe she had been resurrected from hibernation. She stood on her short hind legs. How beautiful she was. For seven years she had been their pet. Jean had trained her, a wild woodchuck, to come into the kitchen and eat melon from her or Shan's hand. Shan was pleased to see her coming out to meet him on his return home.

"I must get out and get to the house to get pecans to feed her," Jean said.

"I have a story to tell you, Jean. I want to tell you what happened to me at Kingston Hospital! I've never told this story to anyone."

"Don't tell me now, I have to get feed for Sugar Lump. . . . Don't tell me your story at all, Shan. You like to write. Write your story for me, Shan!"

About the Author

Jesse Stuart is firmly wedded—not only to Naomi Deane Stuart but to his 1,000-acre corner of heaven on earth in eastern Kentucky. It is an area of rare tranquillity encompassing pastureland, timber, creeks, an abundance of small wildlife. The noises of what we call civilization are notably absent. The occasional cough of a tractor sputtering to life half a mile away is largely blanketed by bird songs and the nattering of mother raccoons scolding their young for misbehavior. Much of Stuart's best writing has stemmed from these same hills and valleys, though he has always been a traveler, both in body and spirit.